The *Ultimate* Kindergarten PREP GUIDE

A complete resource guide with fun and educational activities to prepare your preschooler for kindergarten

Autumn McKay

Find me on Instagram!
@BestMomIdeas

The Ultimate Kindergarten Prep Guide by Autumn McKay
Published by Creative Ideas Publishing

www.BestMomIdeas.com

For permissions contact:
Permissions@BestMomIdeas.com

ISBN: 9781798747209

Table of Contents

About Me

My name is Autumn. I am a wife to an incredible husband, and a mother to two precious boys and a sweet little girl! My children are currently 5 years old, 3 years old and 1 year old.

I have a Bachelor of Science degree in Early Childhood Education. I have taught in the classroom and as an online teacher. I have earned teacher certifications to teach Kindergarten through fifth grade in Arizona, Colorado, California and Georgia. However, one of my greatest joys is being a mom! After my first son was born in 2013, I wanted to be involved in helping him learn and grow, so I began to develop color lessons to help engage his developing mind. I also wanted to help other moms dealing with hectic schedules and continuous time restraints. As a result, these activities evolved into my first book, entitled *Toddler Lesson Plans: Learning Colors*. I continued the daily activities with my son, focusing on learning the alphabet and numbers which turned into *Toddler Lesson Plans: Learning ABC's*. From there I created other activities that I have done with my boys that eventually developed into another book titled *The Ultimate Toddler Activity Guide*.

My oldest son is now 5 years old, and thus the motivation for the book you hold in your hands, *The Ultimate Kindergarten Prep Guide*. As your child prepares for kindergarten, I am confident he or she will benefit from these activities. I have also developed a website called bestmomideas.com to share other activities, as well as tips and tricks of being a mom that I have learned along the way.

Introduction

Preparing for the Kindergarten Year

For a child who will soon enter kindergarten, an activity time offers a wonderful opportunity to prepare him for this transition time by focusing on subject areas he will learn throughout the kindergarten year. The activity time can be used to help build anticipation and excitement about all the fun things he will learn in the upcoming school year. It will also help ease some of the anxiousness he might face beginning a new phase in life (new school, new routine, new friends, and new curriculum).

Education Standards

This book was written to help prepare a preschooler for Kindergarten. In this endeavor, National Education Standards and individual state performance Standards (Massachusetts, Texas, Washington, Georgia, California, Wyoming, Vermont, Florida, and North Dakota) were used as a guide to address fundamental areas of education considered foundational for a child. Each state and school has challenging and clear standards of achievement for each grade level; therefore, various state performance standards were reviewed to help pinpoint key concepts a child needs to know in kindergarten. The topics and themes within this book and the accompanying activities were developed based on the learning goals of these "Education Standards." Even though these "Education Standards" were used as a guideline for developing the activities, an additional focus in creating these activities was to make the learning experience fun and engaging so that learning remains enjoyable for both child and parent.

This book is divided into five different subjects: Math, Language Arts, Science, Social Studies, and Life Skills. At the beginning of each subject area, there is a brief description of what your child will learn by participating in the activities. Please read through the descriptions and activities to determine the best place to begin with your preschooler. You may focus on one subject at a time, working through all the activities in that subject area. Your preschooler may enjoy changing subject areas daily. For example, on Monday do a math activity, on Tuesday do a language arts activity, on Wednesday do a science activity, etc. Please select activities within your child's ability. We want to challenge your child. We want him to enjoy learning. We do not want to frustrate him.

Additional Helpful Hints

Each activity provides a materials list and step-by-step instructions. Each activity's time frame is geared to the attention span of a preschooler; therefore, the activities should only take 10 to 20 minutes. For each activity, I suggest you ask your preschooler if he wants to do a fun activity instead of making him do it. It is very important he continues to enjoy learning. Some days, my boys will tell me they do not want to do an activity, and that is totally fine! However, most days both of my sons will ask when it is activity time. It makes this mommy's heart happy knowing they want to learn!

Although these activities were written to help prepare a preschooler for kindergarten, they can also provide enrichment opportunities throughout the kindergarten school year. As your kindergartener is learning about these topics in his classroom, you can provide hands-on practice at home by doing the activities again. Repetition strengthens the connections in the brain helping these new skills become memories that are easier to recall.

I know many parents are very busy and do not have a lot of time to set up an activity, so I have placed a "low prep" ribbon beside all activities that should only take a minute or two to prep. I hope these low/no prep activities make life a little easier for you, especially on busy days.

To help you prepare your materials in advance, look ahead at the next set of activities you want to do with your preschooler. At this time make a list of all the materials you will need to buy during your next shopping trip to the grocery store.

I try to keep an assortment of school supply items in my house to be used for activities, so I do not constantly have to run to the store. Here is a list of materials used consistently for many of the activities throughout this book if you want to stock up:

☐ Construction Paper
☐ Glue
☐ Crayons
☐ Scissors (adult and toddler)
☐ Paper Plates
☐ Beads
☐ Washable Paint
☐ Paintbrushes

☐ Page Protectors
☐ Dry Erase Markers
☐ Index Cards
☐ Markers
☐ Assortment of Stickers
☐ Food Coloring
☐ Pipe Cleaners
☐ Poster Board

A Gift for You

As noted earlier, one of my books is entitled, *The Ultimate Toddler Activity Guide,* this book has many educational activities, which will be helpful to you in accomplishing some of the learning goals presented in the "Education Standards." In appreciation of your purchase of this book, in the following pages I have placed three links to activities from *The Ultimate Activity Toddler Guide.* These links will lead you to 82 additional activities which will not only assist you in your goal of preparing your child for kindergarten, but should be enjoyable for both you and your preschooler. The links are listed in their appropriate topic areas. However, if you would like to review them at this time, here are the links to the additional activities and the appendix at the back of this book:

www.bestmomideas.com/ultimate-kindergarten-prep-printouts

Password: bestmomideas4k2n

Play Your Way to Learning

Nothing is more charming than a child's face and the many expressions of joy a child exhibits in play and learning. Learning can be so fun! Playtime can be an enjoyable moment for the entire family. Throughout these pages, you will find many wonderful activities which hold the potential to bring a smile to your child's face and joy in your home. My hope is that in the midst of your children "playing their way" to growth and knowledge, this book will help flood your home with joy.

As you begin your journey through this book, I need to mention that in most of the activities I address your child with the pronoun "he." I did this for simplicity and ease of writing; however, please know, as I wrote this book I was thinking of your precious little girl as well. I also want to reiterate that the goal of this book is to provide activities that you can enjoy with your child. The activities in this book are written for the preschooler. However, these years are a time of many developmental milestones. Each child is unique and matures at his or her own pace. If you sense your preschooler is becoming frustrated with an activity, please be sensitive and do not push your child to continue. Without question, you know your child best and what he is capable of attempting. If you feel an activity is beyond your child's present ability, simply move to another activity. There are many great "child tested" activities from which to choose.

Remember, even though significant learning will occur as you engage your child in these activities, I want you and your child to have fun! Often when my preschooler prays, he ends his prayer with the statement, "...And let us have a fun day, Amen." In the midst of hectic days and the constant pressure to perform, a child deserves a fun day. The truth is you deserve a "fun day" as well. It is my desire that in the following pages you will discover a path for your preschooler to learn, and an avenue through which you will experience immense satisfaction as YOU have a fun day and enjoy your child.

I hope these activities bring as much joy and learning to your home as they have mine!

Activities

MATH

According to "Education Standards" for math, a kindergartener's instructional time should focus on learning whole numbers, shapes, and spatial reasoning. By focusing on these concepts, your child will learn how to count in sequence, count the number of objects, and compare numbers. He will also be able to identify and compare shapes. Developing these skills will help a child prepare for simple addition and subtraction, as well as, learning to measure. The following activities address these important topics.

LOW PREP *Number of the Week Chart*

Materials:

☐ Number of the Week Activity Page (Appendix A)
☐ Page Protector
☐ Dry Erase Marker

Directions:

Your preschooler is probably familiar with numbers and counting, but this chart will help him begin to understand a numbers place value, position, addition and subtraction. Place your *Number of the Week* activity page into a page protector. Using the dry erase marker, write the number of the week in the box at the top of the page. Ask your preschooler if he would enjoy learning about the number __ this week. Show him the chart. Ask him to pick one box that he would like to fill out for the day. Let him fill out the box. Fill out one box each day, and place the chart on the refrigerator so your preschooler can reference it throughout the week.

For the "Number Word" box, you can write dotted letters for your preschooler to trace until he becomes familiar with writing letters.

In the "Draw It" box, your preschooler can choose to draw a picture to represent the number of the week. For example, my son likes to draw cars so he would draw two cars to represent the number two.

For the "Tens Frame" box, your preschooler will need to color in the number of boxes to represent the number of the week. He should color boxes from left to right.

In the "More and Less" box, your preschooler will add one to the number of the week, and take away one from the number of the week. Feel free to use fingers or manipulatives, if needed.

On the number line, ask your preschooler to write the number of the week in the center of the number line. Now help him write the two numbers that come before the number of the week on the left and the two numbers that come after the number of the week on the right.

The Ultimate Kindergarten Prep Guide | Autumn McKay

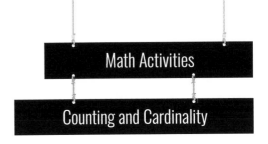
LOW PREP *How Many Dots to Fill a Circle?*

Materials:

- ☐ Eyedropper
- ☐ Paper
- ☐ Marker
- ☐ Page Protector
- ☐ Water
- ☐ Cup
- ☐ Food Coloring (optional)

Directions:

Using your marker, draw circles on a piece of paper. Draw a variety of sizes. Place the piece of paper in a page protector. Fill a cup with water. You can add food coloring for a bit of fun or even have a few cups of colored water.

Ask your preschooler if he would enjoy seeing how many drops of water it takes to fill each circle. Place the circle page in front of your preschooler along with the cup of water and the eyedropper. Explain that he will fill the eyedropper with water by putting the open end of the eyedropper into the water and pinching the rubber end of the eyedropper. Demonstrate how in releasing tension on the rubber bulb, and allowing it to return to its previous shape, water is drawn into the eyedropper. Now, tell him to slowly squeeze the end of the eyedropper between his thumb and index finger to release a drop of water from the eyedropper. Place drops of water into one of the circles and count how many drops it takes to fill it up. Ask him to count out loud as he is filling the circle.

★

LOW PREP *How Many M&M's to Fill a Cup?*

Materials:

- ☐ M&M's
- ☐ Variety of Cups

Directions:

Ask your preschooler if he would like to see how many M&M's it takes to fill a cup. Place several cups of differing sizes in front of your child. Ask him to pick a cup to fill with M&M's. Place a bag of M&M's in front of your preschooler. Tell him to count out loud as he puts each M&M in the cup. This is a great activity for learning to count to 100. Of course, if appropriate, he can enjoy some M&M's after he fills the cup.

Paper Plate Skip Counting

Materials:

☐ Paper Plates
☐ Marker
☐ Single Hole Punch
☐ Yarn

Directions:

Once your preschooler has become very familiar with counting by ones, you can introduce "skip counting." Skip counting is when you count by twos, fives, tens, etc. You can demonstrate how skip counting works by using a number line. Draw a number line on a piece of paper, and then place your finger on the zero. Explain that he will add two to zero to get to the next number—have your finger jump two places to reach the two. Demonstrate it one more time, and then ask your preschooler what number would come next.

I recommend focusing on one skip counting group (twos, fives, or tens) at a time, so it does not confuse or frustrate your child. When you decide which skip counting group to focus on, write that number big in the center of the paper plate. For example, if you choose to count by twos then write a big number two in the center of the paper plate. Now, hole punch 10 holes around the edge of the plate. In a random order, write 2, 4, 6, 8, 10, 12, 14, 16, 18, and 20 below the holes. Using the yarn, tie a knot around the "two hole." Ask your preschooler to take the other end of the yarn and lace it through the number that would come next when counting by twos (the four). Continue this until complete. You can also create skip counting plates for counting by fives and tens.

★

LOW PREP Skip Counting Dot-to-Dot

Materials:

☐ Skip Counting Dot-to-Dot Activity Page (Appendix B)
☐ Pencil or Crayon

Directions:

Ask your preschooler if he would like to do a dot-to-dot activity. Explain to him that instead of counting by ones, he will count by fives to get to the next dot. Review how to count by fives with your preschooler. Show your preschooler the *Skip Counting Dot to Dot* activity page. Show him that he will begin at 5 and then draw a line to the 10, 15, 20, etc. Ask him to continue this process until he reaches 100. When he reaches 100, ask him to color the picture.

Number Hide and Seek

Materials:

☐ Ice Cream Hide and Seek Activity Pages (Appendix C)
☐ Scissors

Directions:

From the activity page, cut out each ice cream top with sprinkles. Now, hide the ice creams around your house.

Ask your preschooler if he would enjoy finding ice cream you have hidden around the house. Show him the *Ice Cream Hide and Seek* activity page with the cones. Explain to him that once he finds an ice cream top, he will need to count how many sprinkles are on the ice cream and then bring it to the cone with the correct number. He will need to find all ten ice creams.

Sometimes I set a timer for games like this because my son enjoys trying to beat the clock, but that is optional.

---------------------- ★ ----------------------

LOW PREP String Beads

Materials:

☐ Pipe Cleaners
☐ Pony Beads

☐ Numbered Flash Cards: 1 through 30

Directions:

On a table, place pipe cleaners, a bowl of pony beads, and a stack of numbered cards. Ask your preschooler to pick a numbered flash card from the stack. Ask him to tell you the number. If your child does not recognize the number, encouragingly tell him. Now ask him to remove that same number of beads from the bowl and string them on a pipe cleaner. Ask him to count out loud as he strings the beads.

Your preschooler can clear off the beads from the pipe cleaner before stringing the next number. However, there is value in placing the beaded pipe cleaner next to the numbered card your child selected, and asking him to select another numbered card. As your child continues with the activity, placing the beaded pipe cleaners alongside each other, he can visually see that each number is represented by differing amounts of beads. I typically continue this activity five or six times before clearing off the pipe cleaners.

LOW PREP Sticker Number Lines

Materials:

- ☐ Sticker Number Line Activity Page (Appendix D)
- ☐ Pencil
- ☐ Small Stickers

Directions:

Fill in the number line on the *Sticker Number Line* activity by writing numbers above each tick on the number line. If your preschooler is just beginning to learn numbers 1-20, write those numbers on the number line. However, if your preschooler is familiar with numbers 1-20, start the number line at 21, 30, or even 50. Please have a sufficient number of stickers available.

Ask your preschooler if he would enjoy counting with stickers. Show him the *Sticker Number Line* activity page. Ask him to point to each number and say it out loud. Provide assistance if needed. Now ask him to start at the first number on the number line and place the corresponding number of stickers. Continue until it is complete, but it's understandable if he needs to take a break and come back to this activity at a later time.

★

LOW PREP Say It, Trace It, Write It

Materials:

- ☐ Say It, Trace It, Write It Activity Page (Appendix E)
- ☐ Pencil

Directions:

Ask your preschooler if he would like to practice writing his numbers. Show him the *Say It, Trace It, Write It* activity page. Explain to him that he will tell you the number first. Next, he will trace the dotted number. Finally, he will practice writing the number himself.

LOW PREP | Count Forward

Materials:

- ☐ Count Forward Activity Page (Appendix F)
- ☐ Pencil

Directions:

Ask your preschooler if he would like to practice counting. Show him the *Count Forward* activity page. Explain to him he will read the number on the left side of the page first. Next, he will need to write the next four consecutive numbers on the lines provided after the number. You can draw dotted numbers for your preschooler if he is still learning to write numbers.

★

Alligator Chomp

Materials:

- ☐ Alligator Chomp Activity Page (Appendix G)
- ☐ Scissors
- ☐ Crayons
- ☐ Household Objects

Directions:

Ask your preschooler if he would like to use an alligator to "chew up" various objects. Explain that he will use the alligator to chomp the bigger groups of objects you set out. Show your preschooler the *Alligator Chomp* activity page. Ask him to color the alligators. When he is finished coloring, he can practice his scissor skills by cutting out the mouths. Please assist your child as needed.

You will need to gather a few groups of household objects from around your house. For example: two bananas, four grapes, six toy cars, three oranges, ten pennies, seven cotton balls, one spoon, etc. Explain to your preschooler that you will place two groups of objects beside each other and he will place an alligator mouth that opens to the bigger group in the center of the objects. Tell your preschooler that the alligator's mouth always wants to eat the bigger number (or group) because it's very hungry.

For example, starting from the left, you can place one spoon on the table, leave a space in the center (enough space for you preschooler to place the alligator mouth) and then place four grapes on the table. Your preschooler should then pick the alligator mouth that opens to the right (in the direction of the four grapes) and place it between the groups of objects. After your preschooler places the alligator mouth, ask him why he chose the alligator mouth that he did.

LOW PREP *More or Less*

Materials:

☐ More or Less Activity Page (Appendix H)
☐ Crayons

Directions:

Ask your preschooler if he would like to compare numbers. Show him the *More or Less* activity page. Explain to him that he will look at the number at the bottom of each column and then color in the corresponding number of squares above the number. After he colors in the first group of numbers, ask him which number is bigger. Ask him to circle the bigger number. Do this for each group of numbers.

★

Comparing Numbers Board Game

Materials:

☐ Comparing Numbers Board Game Activity Pages (Appendix I)
☐ Scissors
☐ 2 Board Game Pieces

Directions:

Ask your preschooler if he would like to play a fun game. Cut out all the squares on the second activity page and shuffle them. Explain to your preschooler that you will each place a board game piece on the start line—these can be coins, buttons, cars, etc. Now you and your preschooler will each flip over a blue square card. Ask your preschooler to count the dots on each square card and decide which square has more dots. The person that flipped over the square card with the most dots is the winner and gets to move one space. Place the cards at the bottom of the stack and continue until a player reaches the finish line.

`LOW PREP` Egg Crate Ten Frames

Materials:

- ☐ Egg Crate
- ☐ Pom Poms
- ☐ Scissors

Directions:

Cut off two of the egg holders from the end of the egg crate to make an egg crate with ten egg holders. With a marker, from left to right, number the top row of egg holders one through five and the bottom row, six through ten.

Ask your preschooler if he would like to do a fun counting activity with pom poms. Tell him that you will call out a number and he will place that number of pom poms in the egg crate. For example, if you call out the number six, he will place one pom pom in each of the egg holders in the top row, and he will place the sixth pom pom in the first egg holder on the bottom row.

★

One More, One Less Fish Bowls

Materials:

- ☐ One More, One Less Fish Bowl Activity Pages (Appendix J)
- ☐ Page Protector or Laminator
- ☐ Dry Erase Marker
- ☐ Scissors

Directions:

Cut out the 30 fish on the second *One More, One Less Fish Bowl* activity page. Laminate the first *One More, One Less Fish Bowl* activity page or place it in a page protector.

Ask your preschooler if he would enjoy adding and subtracting fish. Use the dry erase marker to write a number, 1-10, in the "My Number" column. Ask your preschooler to count that number of fish, and place them in the center fish bowl. Now ask him to tell you what is one less than the "My Number." You can take away one of the fish from the center fish bowl, and let him count the fish to help him calculate the answer. Ask him to write the number under the fish bowl and then place that many fish in the "One Less" fish bowl. Now ask your preschooler what is one more than the "My Number." You may add a fish to the center fish bowl, and let your preschooler count the total to determine the answer, if needed. Ask him to write the number under the "One More" fish bowl. Place that number of fish in the fish bowl. Continue this activity as many times as your preschooler would like.

Finger Math

Materials:

- ☐ Construction Paper
- ☐ Pencil
- ☐ Scissors
- ☐ Glue

Directions:

Ask to trace your preschooler's hands onto construction paper. Cut out the hands. Place the hands on another piece of paper, and ask your preschooler to rub glue on the palms of the hands. Glue the palm of the hands onto the paper. Do not glue the fingers. The fingers should be loose.

On a separate piece of paper write addition problems that add to ten, but leave the answer blank. For example, 3+7=__, 1+9=__, 9+1=__, etc. In helping your child solve the equation, have him lift the same number of fingers that represents the first number of the addition problem. Next, have him lift the number of fingers that represent the second number in the addition problem. Now ask your preschooler to count how many fingers are lifted. This is the sum of the addition problem. He can write his answer in the blank.

When your preschooler is ready to practice subtraction, write out numbers that subtract from ten. Start with all ten fingers lifted, and ask your preschooler to fold down the number of fingers that is written second in the subtraction problem. Now he can count how many fingers are still raised to find the answer to his subtraction problem.

LOW PREP *How Many More to Get to Ten?*

Materials:

- ☐ Egg Crate
- ☐ Pom Poms
- ☐ Scissors

Directions:

Use the same egg crate ten frame from the *Egg Crate Ten Frames* activity. Ask your preschooler if he would like to do a fun adding activity. Explain to him you will call out a number and he will fill in the egg holders with a pom pom. As in the *Egg Crate Ten Frames* activity, there are five egg holders on the top row and five egg holders on the bottom row. Ask your child to place only one pom pom in an egg holder. If the number six is called out, starting at the top left egg holder, the child should place one pom pom in each egg holder on the top row. The sixth pom pom should be placed in the bottom left egg holder.

In this activity, we will include addition and subtraction.

For the addition activity, tell your preschooler a number and have him put the appropriate number pom poms in the egg crate. Now ask him how many more pom poms are needed to equal a total of ten pom poms. Encourage your child to count the pom poms as he places them in the egg holders. After he has solved the addition problem, reinforce the learning experience by stating the entire equation to your child and asking him to repeat what you have said. For example, tell your preschooler to fill in seven egg holders. After he fills in seven egg holders, ask him how many more pom poms are needed to equal a total of ten pom poms. At this point your child will count out three more pom poms (completely filling all the egg holders in the egg crate). Next, state the entire equation, "Seven plus three equals ten." Now, ask your child to verbally repeat the equation to you.

For the subtraction activity, your preschooler will start with all egg holders filled with pom poms. Call out a number less than ten. For example, you might call out the number three. Now ask, "Ten minus three equals what number?" Your preschooler will remove three pom poms from the egg crate. Ask your preschooler to count the number of pom poms remaining in the egg crate. He will count a total of seven pom poms. Now have your preschooler verbally state the subtraction problem with the answer, "Ten minus three equals seven."

LOW PREP *Ladybug Addition*

Materials:

- ☐ Ladybug Addition Activity Page (Appendix K)
- ☐ Pencil
- ☐ Dice

Directions:

Show your preschooler the *Ladybug Addition* activity page. Explain to him he will roll the dice and then draw the same number of dots on the left wing of the ladybug. After he draws the correct number of dots, he will write the number in the first box underneath the ladybug. Next, he will roll the dice again and draw that number of dots on the right wing of the ladybug, and write the number in the second box of the equation. Ask him to count all the dots to get the sum. He can write the sum of the dots in the box after the equal sign. Read the math problem to your preschooler as you point to each number in the problem.

Adding Tubes

Materials:

- ☐ Half a Piece of Poster Board (14 inches by 22 inches)
- ☐ 2 Paper Towel Tubes
- ☐ Tape
- ☐ Marker
- ☐ Paper or Dry Erase Board
- ☐ Counters (Pom Poms, Cotton Balls, Beads, Pennies, etc.)
- ☐ 2 Bowls

Directions:

In creating your adding tubes, lay the poster board in front of you with the longer dimension extending from top to bottom. Now place a paper towel tube on the left side of the poster board, but angle it so that the top of the tube is pointed towards the top left corner of the poster board and the bottom of the tube is pointed towards the center of the bottom edge of the poster board. Tape it in place. Now place a paper towel tube on the right side of the poster board, but again angle it so the top of the tube is pointed to the top right corner of the poster board and the bottom of the tube is pointed towards the center of the bottom edge of the poster board. Tape it in place. The tubes should almost form a "V" on the poster board. Use your marker to draw a big plus sign in between the paper towel tubes. Hang your poster board from the refrigerator or wall and place an empty bowl underneath the paper towel tubes. Place your "counters" in another bowl.

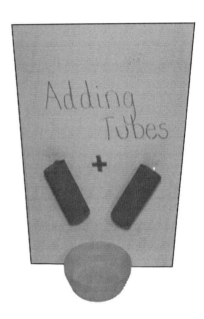

Ask your preschooler if he would enjoy using the adding tubes to do some math. Explain to him that you will write an addition problem on the white board. Using the first number in the addition problem, ask your child to identify the number and count out this number of "counters." Direct your child to place these "counters" in the first tube (the counters should drop into the bowl). Likewise, using the second number in the addition problem, ask your child to identify this number and count out the same number of "counters." Ask your child to place these "counters" in the second tube. All of the counters should fall into the bowl. Now ask your child to calculate the sum of the two numbers by counting all the "counters" in the bowl.

Start with numbers whose sum equals ten or less. After your child becomes proficient at this, you may want to try numbers whose sum totals greater than ten.

LOW PREP *Say It, Make It, Answer It*

Materials:

☐ Say It, Make It, Answer It Activity Page (Appendix L)
☐ Page Protector or Laminator

☐ Counters
☐ Dry Erase Marker
☐ Eraser

Directions:

Either laminate or place your *Say It, Make It, Answer It* activity page in a page protector. Show the activity page to your preschooler. Explain to him that you will write an addition problem in the "Say it" box. He will then read the problem to you. After that, he will use "counters" to make the addition problem in the "Make it" box, by placing the first group of "counters" in the box and then counting out the second group of "counters" and placing them in the box. Finally, he will count the total number of "counters" to find the answer. Once your child calculates the answer, instruct him to use the dry erase marker to write the number in the "Answer it" box.

Do this activity as many times as your preschooler would like. You can also use this activity page to help your preschooler solve subtraction problems.

★

LOW PREP *Addition War*

Materials:

☐ Deck of Cards

Directions:

This is one of my oldest son's favorite games. If it is a new deck of cards, take out the joker cards and shuffle the cards. Next, pass out the cards by handing one to your preschooler and one to yourself until the entire deck in passed out. Keep the cards face down. Now you and your preschooler will each flip over the top two cards from your stacks. Each player should add together the value of the two cards. Be sure to say the addition problem out loud so your preschooler can hear the problem. The person with the higher sum wins all four cards. Play where a Jack is 10 points, Queen is 11 points, King is 12 points and Ace is 1 point.

For instance, if you flipped over a 5 and Queen, you would add 5+11=16. If your preschooler flipped over a King and 2, he would add 12+2=14. Your sum was bigger so you would get all four cards.

If there is a tie score, each player selects an additional card and the new sum is totaled. The person with the highest score wins all six cards. We usually place the winning cards in a new stack to see who gets the most cards by the time we run out of cards to flip over.

Playdough Smash Subtraction

Materials:

- ☐ Index Cards
- ☐ Marker
- ☐ Playdough

Directions:

Prepare this activity by writing subtraction problems on index cards. Keep the subtraction problems ranging with numerals from zero to ten (10-7=, 5-2=, 6-1=, 4-2=, 8-5=, 4-3=, etc.). Now roll out 20 medium to small sized balls from your playdough.

Ask your preschooler if he would enjoy playing a fun "smashing game." Place subtraction problem cards face down in front of your preschooler. Ask him to flip over a card and read it to you. Instruct him to gather the same number of playdough balls as the first number in the problem. Place the balls on the table. Now ask him to read the second number in the problem. He will smash the number of balls equivalent to the second number in the subtraction problem. Ask him how many balls are left. To reinforce learning ask him to state the subtraction problem with the correct answer.

For example, if your preschooler flipped over "5-2=," he would gather five playdough balls and place them on the table in front of him. Next, he would smash two playdough balls and count the remaining balls. Finally, he would state the solved equation, 5-2=3.

Number Line Hop

Materials:

☐ Number Line Hop Activity Page (Appendix M)
☐ Scissors
☐ Page Protector or Laminator
☐ Dry Erase Marker
☐ Eraser

Directions:

Laminate the number line and task cards from the *Number Line Hop* activity page, and cut them out. If you do not have a laminator, cut out the number line and task cards and place them inside a page protector.

Ask your preschooler if he would like to do a bunny math activity. Place the number line in front of your preschooler along with a task card. Read the task card to your preschooler. Explain to him that he will place his dry erase marker on the number the task card says to start on. Next, he will hop forwards or backwards the number of spaces the task card says. Tell him that it only counts as a hop when he reaches the next number, so he will not count the number he starts on. Where he ends his "hopping journey" is the answer to the task card. Finally, ask him to write the answer in the square on the task card. Erase the number line and start over.

For example, if you read the task card, "Start at 2 and hop forward 3 spaces." Ask your preschooler to place the dry erase marker on the number two, and draw a "hop" to three, four, and five. Next, your preschooler should write a number "5" in the box on the task card. Explain to your child that 2+3=5. Erase the number line, and begin again with a new task card. (Two task cards are blank to allow you to select whichever numbers you prefer.)

LOW PREP Subtraction Bowling

Materials:

☐ 10 Toilet Paper Tubes
☐ Medium Size Ball

Directions:

Ask your preschooler if he would enjoy bowling. Place the ten toilet paper tubes in a triangle formation on the floor with one in front, two behind the one, three behind the two, and four behind the three. Make sure they are evenly spaced out. Ask your preschooler to stand back approximately six feet. Explain to him that there are ten pins up and he will need to roll the ball to knock down the pins. After he rolls and knocks down some pins, ask him to count how many he knocked down. Say the math problem to him "10-__=?" inserting the number of pins he knocked down in the equation. Ask him to solve the problem by counting how many pins are still standing. Now state the entire math problem to him, with the answer. Set the pins up and play as many times as your preschooler would like.

For example, if your preschooler knocked down five pins you would say to your preschooler, "Ten minus five equals what number?" Next, you would instruct him to count the remaining standing pins and tell you the answer. Finally, ask him to repeat the math problem with the answer, "Ten minus fives equals five."

LOW PREP ✦ *Word Problems*

Materials:

- ☐ Word Problems Activity Page (Appendix N)
- ☐ Page Protector or Laminator
- ☐ Scissors
- ☐ Dry Erase Marker
- ☐ Eraser

Directions:

Cut out the word problems on the second page of the *Word Problems* activity page. Place one of the cut-outs on the "Read it" box on the first page of the *Word Problems* activity page and place them inside a page protector (or you may laminate the activity pages). Read the word problem to your preschooler. Next, ask him to draw a picture to represent the word problem. Lastly, he can write the math problem in the "Answer it" box and solve the problem.

For example, if the "Read It" word problem is, "My mom made six pancakes for breakfast. I ate two. How many are left?" First, instruct your child to draw six pancakes in the "Draw it" box because that is the number of pancakes which were prepared. Next, ask your child to draw an "X" over the pancakes the child ate. He would cross out two pancakes because the boy ate two pancakes for breakfast. Now he can write, "6-2=" in the "Answer it" box. Finally ask your preschooler to solve the word problem by counting the pancakes which are not "crossed out." He now writes "4" as the answer to the math problem in his "Answer it" box.

Compose Number Bonds

Materials:

- ☐ Construction Paper
- ☐ Glue
- ☐ Scissors
- ☐ Counters

Directions:

Ask your preschooler if he would like to help you make a "Number Bond" to use for two activities. First, let your preschooler practice his cutting skills by cutting a large circle and two medium circles from a piece of construction paper. Next, cut two 2-inch by 11-inch strips from construction paper. Place your two strips of paper to form a "V." Glue them together. Now place your large circle on the "V's" point and place your two medium circles on the ends of the "V." Let your preschooler glue everything in place.

Place "counters" in front of your preschooler. Tell your child a number and ask him to place that number of counters on one of the medium circles. Tell your child another number and have him place the same number of counters on the other medium circle. Now ask him to calculate the sum of the two numbers by sliding the counters from the medium circles to the large circle and counting all of the counters.

For example, you can tell your preschooler to count out six counters and place them in a medium circle. Count out six more counters and place them in the other medium circle. Now he can slide all of the counters from the medium circles to the large circle and count the total number of counters. He should count 12. You can then tell him that 6+6=12. Continue to play this as long as your preschooler wants.

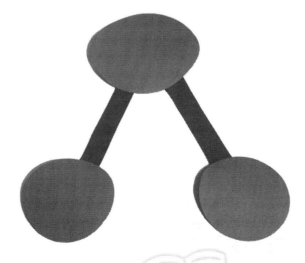

LOW PREP *Decompose Number Bonds*

Materials:

☐ Construction Paper
☐ Glue
☐ Scissors
☐ Counters
☐ Paper
☐ Pencil

Directions:

Use the same "number bond" you and your preschooler created for the *Composing Number Bonds* activity. Start with "counters" in the large circle and ask your child to slide counters into each of the medium circles. This will help show your preschooler that numbers can be broken into a variety of ways.

For example, ask your preschooler to place eight counters in the large circle. Tell him there are many ways the number eight can be broken into two groups. It is his role to split up the number eight by sliding the counters into the medium circles. He may choose to split the eight by making a group of three and five, four and four, one and seven, two and six, or zero and eight—all of these ways are correct.

Use paper and pencil to write down all of the ways your child splits the large number so your child can visually see how many ways there are to split a number. Simply draw the bonds on a piece of paper and let him fill in the numbers as he creates them.

LOW PREP *Grouping with Sticks*

Materials:

- ☐ Craft Sticks
- ☐ Rubber Bands
- ☐ Paper
- ☐ Pencil

Directions:

Explain to your preschooler that sometimes people group numbers together to make it easier to count. Tell him people like to count out groups of ten to help them be able to count by tens. Place the craft sticks in front of your preschooler. Ask him to count out ten craft sticks. After he has counted ten sticks help him wrap a rubber band around the group. Now explain to him that he now knows this group of sticks is ten sticks so when you ask him to count a certain number of sticks he does not have to start at one, he can start at the number ten and count forward.

To help him learn this concept, ask him to give you twelve sticks. He may start grabbing the single sticks to count out twelve. If so, correct him by pointing to the group of ten and ask him how many sticks are in this group. Lay the group of ten in front of him and say, "ten." Next, place a single stick alongside the group and say, "eleven." Finally, place another single stick alongside the group and say, "twelve." Do this several times.

You can also use your paper and pencil to write the numbers 10 through 20 down the edge of the paper. Let your preschooler make groups to represent each number so he can see the numbers and groups visually.

Another fun activity is to play a game with you as the customer. Tell your preschooler he is the store cashier. You come to the store to buy X amount of candy and he has to hand you the correct amount of candy without breaking apart any ten groups.

LOW PREP *Make a Balance Scale*

Materials:

- ☐ Plastic Hanger
- ☐ 2 Plastic Cups
- ☐ String
- ☐ Scissors
- ☐ Hole Punch
- ☐ Variety of Objects to Fit in the Cups

Directions:

Ask your preschooler if he would like to make a balance where he can compare the weight of different objects. Let your preschooler punch two holes at the top of each plastic cup. The holes will be punched on the opposite sides of the cups. Cut two pieces of string 18 inches long. String the yarn through the holes of each cup so the cups look like a basket with a handle. Tie the strings around the holes. Let your preschooler place the strings on the hanger. Now hang the hanger from a doorknob.

Ask your preschooler to find some objects to place in the cups to compare their weight. You can discover if five grapes weigh more than five pennies. You can also ask your preschooler how many goldfish his toy car weighs. To determine the answer, tell him he needs to place his toy car in one cup and then count how many goldfish he places in the other cup until the balance is even. Let your preschooler choose what he wants to compare or weigh.

LOW PREP　Measure Objects with Unifix Cubes

Materials:

☐　Unifix Cubes

Directions:

Ask your preschooler if he would like to measure things around the house. If you do not have Unifix Cubes you can use anything you have: books, bananas, toy cars, crayons, markers, etc. Gather a few objects from around the house and place them in front of your preschooler (shoe, book, kitchen chair, pillow, plate, stuffed toy, etc). Explain to your preschooler that he will need to place the Unifix Cubes beside the object he is measuring. He can add more cubes or take away cubes. The goal is for the cubes and the object to be the same length. Now, ask your child to count the number of cubes.

For example, if your preschooler was measuring a book. He would place a Unifix cube at the book's edge and continue to add Unifix Cubes until the cubes and top of the book are even. Next, your preschooler counts how many cubes it took to measure the book.

It is also fun to cut different lengths of string for your preschooler to measure using Unifix Cubes.

──────────── ★ ────────────

LOW PREP　Measure Objects with a Ruler

Materials:

☐　Measuring Activity Page (Appendix O)　　☐　Pencil
☐　Ruler (Optional)

Directions:

Ask your preschooler if he would like to measure with a ruler. Place the *Measuring* activity page in front of him. Tell him the ruler measures in inches. Also explain that to measure an object, the object must be placed at the end of the ruler or at the "0" line on the ruler. From that point, you can see how far it stretches across the ruler.

Show your preschooler a real ruler if you have one. Show him the inches side of the ruler and the centimeters side. Let him practice measuring his pencil by placing the eraser at the beginning of the ruler and laying it flat along the edge of the ruler. Show your preschooler how to find the measurement in inches.

Now explain to your preschooler he will measure different objects on his *Measuring* activity page. Show him that all the objects are lined up at the beginning of the rulers and he will need to see how far they stretch across the ruler. After each measurement, ask him to write his answer on the line.

LOW PREP Order by Size

Materials:

- ☐ Order by Size Activity Page (Appendix P)
- ☐ Ruler (Optional)
- ☐ Scissors
- ☐ Glue

Directions:

Show your preschooler the *Order by Size* activity page. Ask him to cut out each sunflower and glue them in order from shortest to tallest. He may then color the sunflowers.

After he completes this task, you can add a bonus step by asking him to measure each sunflower using a ruler. Ask him to write the answer above the sunflower.

★

LOW PREP Compare Family Members' Heights

Materials:

- ☐ Family Members' Heights Activity Page (Appendix Q)
- ☐ Family Members
- ☐ Tape Measure
- ☐ Pencil

Directions:

Ask your preschooler if he would like to measure the height of each family member. Give your preschooler a tape measure and ask him to pull it across the floor to 84 inches (7 feet). Lock the tape measure in place. One at a time, ask family members to lay next to the tape measure, so your preschooler can measure each family member's height in inches. Remind your preschooler to line up the beginning of the tape measure with the end of the family member's feet to be able to obtain an accurate measurement. After your preschooler has measured a family member, have him write the family member's name on the chart on the *Family Members' Heights* activity page along with the measurement. Do this for each family member. Next, read the statements to your preschooler and ask him to fill in the answers for each statement.

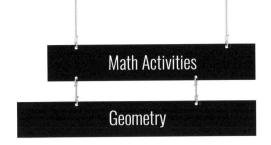
LOW PREP
Build Marshmallow Shapes

Materials:

☐ Mini Marshmallows
☐ Toothpicks

Directions:

Ask your preschooler if he would like to make two-dimensional and three-dimensional shapes out of marshmallows. Demonstrate to your child how to safely use marshmallows and toothpicks to create different shapes. For example, he can create a triangle by sticking two toothpicks into a marshmallow at a 45-degree angle. Add a marshmallow to each end of the toothpicks and stick a toothpick between the marshmallows to connect them.

Assist your preschooler in making a variety of shapes: square, triangle, cube, triangular prism, pyramid, pentagon, hexagon, octagon, etc. In addition, encourage him to create his own shapes.

★

3D Shape Puzzles

Materials:

☐ 3D Shape Puzzles Activity Page (Appendix R)
☐ Scissors
☐ Laminator (Optional)

Directions:

Cut out all of the puzzle pieces from the *3D Shape Puzzle* activity page. If possible, laminate them so you can use them multiple times. Ask your preschooler if he would like to put together puzzles.

Shuffle the puzzle pieces and spread them out in front of your preschooler. Ask him to pick a piece. Ask him what shape is in the picture. If he isn't sure, tell him. Next, ask him to find the matching shape and connect the pieces together. Do this for each shape.

LOW PREP Shape Hunt

Materials:

☐ Shape Hunt Activity Page (Appendix S)
☐ Pencil

Directions:

Ask your preschooler if he would enjoy going on a scavenger hunt. Show him the *Shape Hunt* activity page and explain that together you will walk around the house or outside and look for objects that have the same shape as the picture in the left column. When he finds a shape, ask him to draw the object he found in the box to the right of the shape.

Review each shape in the left column with your preschooler before you begin your hunt. It is helpful to guide your preschooler toward objects that match the shapes until he understands the rules of the game.

Examples of shapes we found around our house are: circle-plate, square-picture frame, triangle-yield sign, rectangle-piece of paper, oval-beans, rectangular prism-tissue box, cube-block, sphere-ball, cone-party hat, and cylinder-battery.

★

LOW PREP Make a Shape Character

Materials:

☐ Shape Character Activity Page (Appendix T)
☐ Pencil
☐ Crayons

Directions:

Ask your preschooler if he would like to draw his own shape character. Show him the *Shape Character* activity page. Explain that he can use all or some of the shapes at the bottom of the page to draw an animal, robot, monster, house, or anything he would like. After he draws and colors his picture, ask him to circle the shapes at the bottom of the page that he included. For a challenge, ask him to count how many of each shape he included in his drawing.

It is also fun to draw a character while your preschooler is drawing his character. Afterwards, ask your preschooler to find the different shapes you included in your drawing.

LOW PREP Make 3D Shapes

Materials:

- ☐ 3D Shapes Activity Pages (Appendix U)
- ☐ Scissors
- ☐ Glue or Tape

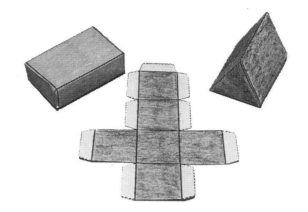

Directions:

Ask your preschooler if he would enjoy turning a flat piece of paper into 3D shapes. You or your preschooler will need to cut out each shape pattern from the *3D Shapes* activity pages. Ask your preschooler which shape he would like to make first. Explain to him that he will need to fold each tab (dotted line) inward. Next, he will fold along any solid lines to help each shape form. Rub glue along each tab and begin to fold the shape to form a 3D shape. Make sure you tuck the tabs under the shape's edges.

★

LOW PREP Position Word Drawing

Materials:

- ☐ Paper
- ☐ Crayons

Directions:

Ask your preschooler if he would like to draw some bugs. Hand your preschooler a piece of paper and ask him to draw a big leaf on his paper. Now explain to him that you will ask him to draw different colored bugs around his leaf and he will need to listen closely to hear what color bug he needs to draw and where to place his bug on the paper.

Be creative with the directions, but here is an example of what to ask your preschooler to draw:

"Draw a red bug on top of the leaf. Draw a blue bug above the leaf. Draw a brown bug below the leaf. Draw a yellow bug next to the leaf. Draw a green bug under the leaf (this one is tricky, and he will not have to draw anything). Draw a purple bug beside the leaf. Draw a black bug on the leaf."

LOW PREP *Position Word Game*

Materials:

☐ Position Word Game Activity Page (Appendix V)
☐ Scissors

Directions:

Cut out the game cards from the *Position Word Game* activity page. Shuffle the cards. Ask your preschooler if he would enjoy playing a game. Explain to him that you will read a card, and he will need to listen carefully and do what is requested on the card. Play as long as your preschooler wants.

LANGUAGE ARTS

The English Language Arts Standards are developed to use as a stepping-stone in each grade level. As your child progresses through grade school, his reading ability, comprehension skills, writing skills, and understanding of the English language should strengthen each year as he practices those skills. To help master these skills, it is beneficial to focus on foundational skills such as: learning the parts of a book, how to follow words, parts of a story, beginning stages of reading, and writing skills. The following activities will help your child develop in each of these important areas.

LOW PREP *Parts of a Book*

Materials:

☐ Favorite Book

Directions:

Ask your preschooler if he would like to learn about the different parts of a book. Let him pick out his favorite book. Point to the front cover of the book and tell him it is the front cover. Show him the title of the book on the front cover. If the author and illustrator's names are on the front cover, point to those and read them to him. Explain to your preschooler that an author writes the story and an illustrator draws the pictures. Turn the book over and show him the back cover of the book.

Open the book up to the title page and tell your preschooler the title page lists the title of the book, the author, and illustrator of the book. Turn to the first page of the book. Ask your preschooler to point to the top of the page. Ask him to point to the bottom of the page. Ask your preschooler if he can point to a letter on the page, a word, and a sentence. Explain to him that letters make up a word and when you put words together they make a sentence.

Explain to him that to read the words on a page you always start at the top, left side of the page. As you read the words to him scroll your finger under the words so he can gain a sense of how to read. Now, point out the spaces between words and sentences. Explain that the space is there so you know it is a new word or sentence and can take a breath. Feel free to practice these print concepts each time you read a book.

LOW PREP *Letter, Word, Sentence Sort*

Materials:

☐ Letter, Word, Sentence Sort Activity Pages (Appendix W)
☐ Scissors
☐ Glue
☐ Crayons

Directions:

Show your preschooler the *Letter, Word, Sentence Sort* activity pages. Explain to him that he will cut out each square on the second activity page, and then he will place them into the correct group. Ask your preschooler to point to a letter on the activity page. Ask him to point to a word. Ask him to point to a sentence.

All the letters will go in the top four boxes. All the squares with a single word will go in the middle four boxes. All the squares with sentences will go in the bottom four boxes. Ask your child to glue them in the correct place. After he glues the squares in place, he can color the pictures.

★

LOW PREP *Connect Upper and Lowercase Letters*

Materials:

☐ Connect Upper and Lowercase Letters Activity Pages (Appendix X)
☐ Pencil or Crayon

Directions:

Ask your preschooler if he would enjoy matching uppercase and lowercase letters together. Since this activity has several pages, I recommend doing one page a day unless your preschooler asks to do more. Show him the first *Connect Upper and Lowercase Letters* activity page. Explain to him that all the letters on the left side are uppercase letters and all the letters on the right side are lowercase letters. The goal is to look at the letter on the left side and find its lowercase match on the right side. Once he finds the match, he can draw a line to connect the two letters. Do this for each letter. Assist your preschooler with finding the lowercase letters if this is his first time being introduced to lowercase letters, but let him guess the match first.

Spoon Matching

Materials:

- ☐ 26 White Plastic Spoons
- ☐ 26 Clear Plastic Spoons
- ☐ Marker

Directions:

Write an uppercase letter towards the top edge of each white plastic spoon. Write a lowercase letter towards the bottom of the spoon, close to the handle, on each clear plastic spoon. When the clear spoon is placed on top of the white spoon both letters should be seen.

Ask your preschooler if he would enjoy playing a fun matching game. Tell him you have upper and lowercase letters written on spoons. Ask him to pick a white spoon with an uppercase letter. Next, ask him to find the matching lowercase letter in the clear plastic spoons, to lay on top of the spoon with the uppercase letter. This game can be played many times.

★

LOW PREP # Dot the Rhyme

Materials:

- ☐ Dot the Rhyme Activity Page (Appendix Y)
- ☐ Do-A-Dot Markers or Markers

Directions:

Ask your preschooler if he would enjoy finding words that rhyme. Tell him rhymes are words that sound alike. Give him a few examples like clock and sock, or car and star. Ask him, if he can tell you a rhyme.

Show your preschooler the *Dot the Rhyme* activity page. Point to the picture on the left side of the page, and ask him to tell you what is in the picture. Say the name of the picture. Explain that he will need to pick one of the three pictures on the right side that rhymes with the one on the left. When he finds the rhyming pictures, tell him to use his Do-A-Dot marker to place a dot on it. If you do not have Do-a-Dot markers, he can use a marker or crayon to color in the picture. Do this for each rhyme.

Erase Me Rhyme

Materials:

☐ Dry Erase Board or Page Protector and Piece of Paper
☐ Dry Erase Markers

Directions:

On a dry erase board, draw a detailed picture illustrating the appropriate parts of the body (or clothing) needed for this activity (see below). If you do not have a dry erase board, simply slide a piece of paper into a page protector and draw the person on top of the page protector. Windows also work as great dry erase boards.

After you have drawn your person, ask your preschooler if he wants to play a silly rhyming game. Explain to him that you will say a rhyme and he will need to decide what part of the person rhymes with your rhyme. Put emphasis on the bold words in each rhyme so he will know what word he needs to rhyme. If needed, point to the correct part of your body to help guide your preschooler to the correct rhyming word. When your child states the correct rhyming word (hair, hand, ear, etc.) tell him to erase that part of the person. Begin to read the rhymes to your preschooler:

Why is there a bear in a **chair** sitting in my _____? (hair)

I think that **sand** might **land** right in my _____. (hand)

I **rant**, did someone put **ants** in my _____. (pants)

Oh **dear**, do you **hear** that bee **near** my _____. (ear)

Bye little flies. I think it is **wise** for me to close my ____. (eyes)

Sound the **alarm**. There is a monkey on my ____. (arm)

Get the **hose** and clean this **rose** off my ____. (nose)

Did you hear the **news**? I have **two** new blue ____. (shoes)

A breeze blew from the **south** blowing dust right into my ____. (mouth)

I ate some **smelly jelly** that went straight to my ____. (belly)

Rhyming Matching Game

Materials:

- ☐ Rhyming Matching Game Activity Page (Appendix Z)
- ☐ Scissors
- ☐ Construction Paper
- ☐ Glue

Directions:

Glue the *Rhyming Matching Game* activity page on to construction paper so the pictures are face up on the construction paper. The construction paper helps prevent your seeing through the cards. Next, cut out all of the squares from the activity page. Shuffle the cards. Lay the cards face down in rows on a table.

Ask your preschooler if he would like to play a rhyming game. Explain to him you have a collection of cards displaying pictures of items that sometimes rhyme. Tell him to select two cards to flip over. Tell you preschooler (verbally say the word) the name of the item pictured on each card. If they rhyme, place them in a pile to the side and ask your preschooler to go again. If they do not rhyme, he will need to flip them back over. Now it is your turn to select two cards. Play until all of the rhymes are found. Whoever has the most matches wins!

Syllable Jump

Materials:

- ☐ Syllable Cards Activity Pages (Appendix AA)
- ☐ Painter's Tape

Directions:

To get your preschooler ready to read, he needs to become aware of the sounds within words. This is called phonological awareness. In helping your child become aware of these sounds, you will teach your preschooler how to break words into syllables. Syllables are the groups of sounds that make up the word. For example, "butterfly" can be broken into three syllables "but-ter-fly."

For this activity, use painter's tape to make a numbered ladder on the floor. Start by laying a piece of painter's tape horizontal in front of your preschooler. Above that piece of tape, use tape to make a number one. Place another piece of tape horizontal above the number one. Next, use the tape to make a number two above the horizontal piece. Continue this until you make a number four. Now, cut out the cards from the *Syllable Cards* activity pages, and shuffle them up.

Ask your preschooler if he would like to play a game. Tell him you will hold up a card. He will look at the picture on the card, say the word, and then say the word slowly while breaking the word into syllables. As he says each syllable, he will take one jump. When he finishes the word, he will look down to see how many syllables it has. Show him an example by using the word "butterfly."

Another way I teach my child to count syllables is to put his hand under his chin and say the word slowly. Each time his chin goes down, while saying the word, it is a syllable. So, when his chin goes down, he jumps.

Here is an answer key:

One Syllable Words-dog, fish, web, stop, key, love, ice, car

Two Syllable Words-mitten, zebra, rocket, hammer, bacon, baby, carrot, ocean

Three Syllable Words-bumblebee, computer, basketball, spaghetti, ladybug, bicycle, umbrella, elephant

Four Syllable Words-calculator, alligator, helicopter, watermelon, rhinoceros, avocado, astronomer, pepperoni

LOW PREP Syllable Picture Sort

Materials:

- ☐ Syllable Cards Activity Pages (Appendix AA)
- ☐ 4 Pieces of Paper
- ☐ Marker

Directions:

In the center of each piece of paper write a number. Write one, two, three, and four. Ask your preschooler if he would like to play a syllable game. Lay each numbered piece of paper in front of your preschooler. Explain to him that you will hold up a card from the *Syllable Cards* activity pages, and he will decide how many syllables are in the word. He can count on his fingers or place his hand under his chin as he says the word. Once he decides how many syllables are in the word, he will place the card on the correct numbered piece of paper.

Please reference *Syllable Jump* activity for an answer key.

★

LOW PREP Syllable Count

Materials:

- ☐ Syllable Count Activity Page (Appendix AB)
- ☐ Counters (coins, manipulatives, M&M's, etc.)

Directions:

Ask your preschooler if he would like to help you count syllables in words. Show him the *Syllable Count* activity page. Explain to him that he will look at the picture and then place a "counter" in the boxes under the picture each time he hears a syllable in the word. After saying the word's final syllable, ask him how many syllables are in the word. Tell him he can find the answer by adding the number of counters he laid down. Do the first one together as an example. Instruct him to use the hand under the chin trick if this would be helpful to him.

Here is an answer key:

1 Syllable Words-bird, drum

2 Syllable Words-bathtub, monkey

3 Syllable Words-octopus, banana

4 Syllable Words-motorcycle, excavator

Syllable Object Sort

Materials:

- ☐ Toys from Around the House
- ☐ 4 Pieces of Paper
- ☐ Marker

Directions:

Write a big number one, two, three, and four in the middle of each paper. Only one number is written on each paper. Place the pieces of paper on the floor. Gather a bucket of various toys and objects from around your home. Objects might include: toy cars, banana, apple, teddy bear, crayon, sunglasses, bracelet, etc.

Explain to your preschooler that he will reach inside the bucket and grab something out of it. He will pull it out and say the name of the object. Next, he will count how many syllables are in the word. When he determines how many syllables are in the word, he places the object on the piece of paper with the correct number.

For example, if your preschooler pulled the teddy bear out of the bucket, he says, "teddy bear." Next, he places his hand under his chin, slowly saying the words, "teddy bear," while counting the syllables. Each time his chin drops, it is a syllable. Since there are three syllables in the words teddy bear, "te-ddy-bear" your preschooler would place the teddy bear on the number three piece of paper.

Sound Matching Game

Materials:

- ☐ Small Container
- ☐ Rice
- ☐ Assortment of Toys
- ☐ Construction Paper
- ☐ Marker

Directions:

You will need to go on a hunt around your house for various small toys that each begin with a different letter of the alphabet. (Skip any letter which is difficult to find). After you have gathered the toys, write the beginning letter of each toy's name on the construction paper. Write the letters in uppercase format. Place approximately 12 letters on one piece of paper. (Of course, the size of the toys will dictate how many letters you can write on a piece of paper). Space the letters apart from each other, so your objects can be placed on the paper without covering multiple letters. Dump all the toys in your small container and pour rice over them.

Ask your preschooler if he would like to go on a hunt. Place the container of rice-covered toys in front of him. Place the papers with letters next to him. Instruct him to dig through the rice to find a toy. After removing the toy from the container, ask your child to slowly say the name of the toy to determine the first letter of the toy's name. Next, ask him to place his toy on the piece of paper, on top of the appropriate letter.

For example, if your preschooler pulled out a key, he would say, "key." Next, he would slowly sound out the word "key" to help him decide the word starts with the letter "K." Finally, he will place the key on the letter "K" on the construction paper and begin again.

LOW PREP · *First Sound Match Up*

Materials:

☐ First Sound Match Up Activity Page (Appendix AC)
☐ Magnetic Letters

Directions:

Ask your preschooler if he would like to match letters to pictures. Show him the *First Sound Match Up* activity page. Ask him to pick out a picture on the page. Ask him to say the name of the picture. Ask your preschooler to say the name slowly so he can listen to the first sound of the word. If needed, assist your child by saying the word slowly emphasizing the first letter sound. When he determines the first letter of the word, ask him to find the letter in the magnetic letters, and place the letter on top of the picture. Do this for each picture.

If you do not have magnetic letters, place the activity page in a page protector and ask your preschooler to write the letter on top of the picture using a dry erase marker.

★

LOW PREP · *Ending Sound*

Materials:

☐ Ending Sound Activity Page (Appendix AD)
☐ Pencil

Directions:

Tell your preschooler that he will be finding the ending sound of words. Show him the *Ending Sound* activity page. Explain to him that he will look at the picture to the left of the word and say the word. Ask him to say it slowly so he can hear the ending sound. If needed, you can help him by saying the word slowly and emphasizing the ending sound. When he determines the ending sound, ask him to write it in the blank. Do this for each picture.

LOW PREP *Doggie, Where's My Bone?*

Materials:

☐ Doggie, Where's My Bone? Activity Pages (Appendix AE)
☐ Scissors

Directions:

Cut out the bone from the second *Doggie, Where's My Bone?* activity page. Place the dog from the activity page in front of your preschooler. Explain to him that you will say a word and then ask him to find a sound in that word. The sound will be at the beginning, middle, or end of the word and he will need to determine where it is. If he hears the sound at the beginning of the word, he will place the bone on the dog's head. If he hears the sound in the middle of the word, he will place the bone on the dog's body. If he hears the sound at the end of the word, he will place the bone on the dog's tail.

Give him an example. Tell him the word "hat" and ask him to find the /a/ sound. Say the word "hat" slowly emphasizing each sound in the word, like /h/-/a/-/t/. He should determine that the /a/ sound is in the middle of the word "hat," so he will need to place the bone on the dog's body.

Here is a list of words to call out to your preschooler: hat, cat, bat, run, fun, wet, bed, mug, pig, big, sit, rat, map, tap, dog, log, rug, bug, tug, wig, hug, fat, cab, mad, sad, dad, and mom.

LOW PREP *Bead Slide*

Materials:

☐ String
☐ Scissors
☐ Beads

Directions:

Ask your preschooler if he would like to make a bracelet. Measure a piece of string that can fit around your preschooler's wrist. Tie a knot in one end of the string. Let your preschooler slide ten beads onto the string. Tie another knot in the other end of the string. Ask your preschooler to push all the beads to the top knot. Explain to your preschooler that you are going to say a word and then together you will sound out the word. Each time he hears a sound in the word he will slide a bead from the top knot to the bottom knot.

For example, "bed" will have three different sounds, "/b/-/e/-/d/." So your preschooler would slide a bead for the /b/ sound, the /e/ sound, and one for the /d/ sound.

Here are some words you can practice together: go, in, be, me, and, dad, mom, ham, cat, net, ant, big, hit, mad, rip, dig, fit, nut, beg, dog, fed, hot, kiss, bat, book, cop, sun, bed, bug, job, sheep, fan, cup, pot, gum, cap, crab, lamp, slim, drop, drum, hunt, black, swim, flop, bump, dust, flag, sand, spin, stop, jump, band, clip, spot, rust, sleep, crop, snug, and plug.

LOW PREP Label Parts of a Book

Materials:

- ☐ Parts of a Book Activity Page (Appendix AF)
- ☐ Scissors
- ☐ Glue

Directions:

Ask your preschooler if he would like to learn the parts of a book. Show him the *Parts of a Book* activity page. Explain to him that he will need to cut out each word from the bottom of the page. Next, he will place the words in the correct box to label each part of the book. Before he cuts out the words, point to each word and read it to your preschooler.

After he finishes cutting out the words, ask him to pick one of the words. Read it together. Ask him to place the word in the correct box that points to the part of the book. For instance, if he picked up "back cover," he would place the word in the top left-hand box that points to the back cover. Do this for each word. Once each word is placed in the correct box, ask him to glue the words in place.

★

LOW PREP Fiction vs. Nonfiction

Materials:

- ☐ Fiction vs. Nonfiction Activity Page (Appendix AG)
- ☐ Scissors
- ☐ Glue
- ☐ Crayons

Directions:

Ask your preschooler if he would enjoy learning what the words fiction and nonfiction mean. Begin by explaining that fiction refers to a book that is make-believe and pretend. Nonfiction refers to a book that is about real facts, real people, or real things that happen. Show your preschooler a real example of each book. Let him look through the books and ask questions.

Show your preschooler the *Fiction vs. Nonfiction* activity page. Explain to him that he will cut out the books along the right side of the page. Together with your child, read the title of the books and ask him to decide if the book is fiction and pretend, or nonfiction and real. When he decides if the book is fiction or nonfiction, have him place the book in the correct box. Now ask him to glue the titles in the boxes. Encourage your child to develop and design his own fiction and nonfiction books.

LOW PREP # Make a Pizza Sequencing

Materials:

- ☐ Pizza Ingredients
- ☐ Oven
- ☐ Paper
- ☐ Pencil

Directions:

Ask your preschooler if he would enjoy making a pizza! Explain to him that you will make a pizza together, but as you make it you will write down each step you take to make the pizza. Explain to him that writing down each step will help him remember how to make the pizza in the correct order the next time he wants to make one. Tell him when you read a story it helps to write down important things that happen in the story so you can remember the story in the correct order.

Ask him what he thinks is the very first step in making a pizza. Let him answer. If he guesses correctly, give him a high five. If your preschooler needs help, tell him the first step is to gather ingredients. Allow your preschooler to watch you as you write "step one" on the piece of paper. Now ask your preschooler to help you gather all the ingredients for the pizza. Ask your preschooler what he thinks "step two" would be. If he guesses correctly, give him another high five. If he needs some guidance, tell him step two is to wash your hands. Together, write step two on your piece of paper. Continue this method as you make your pizza. Once your pizza is in the oven cooking, review all the steps with your preschooler. Ask your preschooler to tell you the steps he can remember. Enjoy your delicious pizza together!

LOW PREP *How to Build a Snowman*

Materials:

☐ How to Build a Snowman Activity Pages (Appendix AH)
☐ Scissors
☐ Glue

Directions:

Ask your preschooler if he would like to build a snowman. Show him the *How to Build a Snowman* activity pages. Explain to him that he will need to cut out each snowman square. Next, you will work to build a snowman by putting the pictures in order from first to last.

After he cuts out each picture, ask him which picture comes first in building a snowman. He should pick the single snowball picture. Ask him to place it in the first square. Now ask him what comes next. He should pick the three snowballs beside each other. Ask him to place it in the second square. Continue this pattern until he completes the activity pages. Once he has all his snowmen pictures in the correct squares, ask him to glue them in place.

★

LOW PREP *Picture Walk*

Materials:

☐ Favorite Book or New Book

Directions:

Ask your preschooler if he would like to take a "picture walk" through a book. Let your preschooler pick a book. (We enjoy doing this activity after we have just checked out books from the library.)

Sit down with your preschooler and explain to him that you are not going to read the words in the book. Instead, you both will look at the pictures in the book and try to guess what the pictures are telling you about the story. Let your preschooler study each picture. Ask him questions about what he sees, what the characters are doing, and what he thinks will happen next.

After you complete a picture walk through of the book, read the book together and discover if your guesses were correct.

LOW PREP *Sticky Note Retelling*

Materials:

☐ Favorite Book
☐ Post-It Notes
☐ Crayons or Pencil

Directions:

Explain to your preschooler he will be working on retelling a story to you. Let him pick a book. Tell him you will read the beginning of the book, and then he will draw a picture on a Post-It note to show what happened in the beginning of the book. You may review what happened in the beginning of the book by asking him questions about the characters or what happened. Next, you will read the middle of the book. He will again draw a picture to show what happened in the middle of the book. Lastly, read the end of the book, and ask him to draw a picture to show what happened at the end of the book. After you finish reading the entire book and he has drawn all his pictures, ask him to tell you what happened in the book. Allow him to refer to his pictures to remember what happened.

This is a great activity to do repeatedly to help build your preschoolers comprehension skills. Once your preschooler is comfortable with retelling the story this way and needs a challenge, try reading the entire book in one sitting. Afterwards, place three Post-It notes in front of your preschooler labeled beginning, middle, and end. Ask him to draw what happened in the beginning of the story on the beginning Post-It note. Next, ask him to draw what happened in the middle of the story on the Post-It note labeled middle. Finally, ask him to draw what happened at the end of the story on the Post-It note labeled end.

Retelling Slider

Materials:

- ☐ Retelling Slider Activity Page (Appendix AI)
- ☐ Scissors
- ☐ Single Hole Punch
- ☐ Pipe Cleaner
- ☐ Pony Bead
- ☐ Favorite Book

Directions:

Cut out the bookmark from the *Retelling Slider* activity page. Punch a hole in the circles at the top and bottom of the bookmark. Slide one pony bead onto a pipe cleaner. Place the pipe cleaner on the left side of the bookmark. Tuck the ends of the pipe cleaner through the holes on the bookmark.

Ask your preschooler if he would like to choose a book to read. Explain to him that as you read, he needs to listen carefully to be able to remember what happens at the beginning, middle, and end of the story. Read the story two or three times to help build your preschoolers confidence in remembering what happens.

After you have read the story, show your preschooler the bookmark you have prepared for this activity. Explain to him that you will ask him to tell you the characters of the story, where the story happened, the beginning of the story, the middle of the story, and the end of the story. Each time he tells you one of the parts of the story he will slide the bead down the bookmark. Start with the bead up at the characters. Ask him to tell you who was in the story. Let him try to remember, but if he needs guidance you may help. When he completes the characters, let him slide the bead down to setting. Continue this for each part of the story.

This is a wonderful activity to do multiple times to build reading comprehension skills!

LOW PREP Story Map

Materials:

☐ Story Map Activity Page (Appendix AJ)   ☐ Crayons
☐ Favorite Book

Directions:

Ask your preschooler if he would like to make a map of his favorite book. Ask him to pick out a book. Read the book to your child. Show him the *Story Map* activity page. Explain to him that he will draw a picture of the characters from the story. Next, he will draw a picture of the setting or where the story happened. Finally, he will draw a picture of the beginning, middle, and end of the story.

It is helpful to do the *Sticky Note* activity as you read through the book, placing Post-It notes in the beginning, middle, and end boxes. Remember to ask your preschooler to describe the picture he drew on the Post-it note depicting his description of the beginning, middle, and end of the book.

★

LOW PREP Who, What, Where, When

Materials:

☐ Who, What, Where, When Activity Page (Appendix AK)
☐ Favorite Book
                              ☐ Crayons

Directions:

Ask your preschooler if he would like to read a book with you. Explain that you will read the book together, and then he will get to answer some questions on a fun-folding page.

Read the book together.

Show your preschooler the *Who, What, Where, When* activity page. Direct him to cut out the big square. Next, he will flip the square face down so the words can't be seen. Now fold the corners back towards the center of the square. At this point the words should be visible.

Ask him to pick a flap. Read the word on the flap. For example, if he picked "Who?" he would answer who was in the story. He would need to lift the flap up and draw a picture of the characters, or write the characters' names. Do this for each flap, answering questions from the story.

◆ **LOW PREP** ◆ *Rhythmic Writing Tracing*

Materials:

☐ Rhythmic Writing Tracing Activity Page (Appendix AL)
☐ Pencil

Directions:

Rhythmic writing is sometimes used to help strengthen processing skills and handwriting. Rhythmic writing is writing done in a fluid motion without ever picking up the pencil.

Ask your preschooler if he would like to trace some silly lines. Show your preschooler the *Rhythmic Writing Tracing* activity page. Explain to him that he will trace the silly lines without picking up his pencil. Show him how to start on the first "c" grouping. He will start on the left side and go up to the top of the "c." Instruct your child to trace back over the line he just made, tracing around the bottom curve of the "c." The movement is very similar to writing a cursive "c."

To help develop your child's processing skills, have him state the direction his pencil is moving or the position of his hand. For example, as he is drawing the "c" grouping have him say, "go up, back around, and down." Make sure his hand matches the directions he is stating at the time he is stating it.

★

Push Pin Maze

Materials:

☐ Cardboard
☐ Push-Pins
☐ Pencil or Crayons

Directions:

Assemble the push-pin maze by cutting out a square or rectangle from an old box. It is a good idea to cut out two of the same size shapes and tape them together around the edges for extra thickness. This provides safety from little fingers getting poked by the push-pins. Once you have your cardboard assembled, place a piece of paper over the cardboard, and design a maze using push-pins. You can create zigzags, shapes, squiggly lines, a straight line to weave in and out, or anything.

Show your preschooler your push-pin maze and ask him if he would like to trace around the maze. Explain where he needs to start, the direction he needs to go, and if there are any special rules. Let your preschooler use a pencil or crayon to complete the maze.

You can do this activity many times by taking the push-pins out of the paper and replacing it with a new piece of paper and push-pin design.

LOW PREP Erase Letters on a Whiteboard

Materials:

- ☐ Whiteboard
- ☐ Dry Erase Markers

Directions:

Ask your preschooler if he would like to erase letters instead of writing them. If you do not have a whiteboard, you can use a window, or place a piece of paper in a page protector. Write a single uppercase letter on the whiteboard. Ask your preschooler to follow the lines to erase it. He should be tracing the letters as he erases it. This will help him develop his writing skills and ability to form letters.

For example, if you drew an uppercase "A," ask him to start at the bottom left side of the "A" and follow the line up, then go down to the bottom right side of the "A." Pick his finger up and drag it across the center line. Do this until your preschooler wants to do something else.

★

LOW PREP Squishy Bag Writing

Materials:

- ☐ Ziploc Gallon Size Bag
- ☐ 1 Cup of Flour
- ☐ ¼ Cup of Water
- ☐ Food Coloring
- ☐ Mixing Bowl
- ☐ Spoon
- ☐ Tape

Directions:

Ask your preschooler if he would like to make a squishy bag. Ask your preschooler to pour the flour into a mixing bowl. Let him pick a food coloring to add to the flour. Add water to the flour mixture. Ask your preschooler to stir the mixture together. Scoop the mixture into the Ziploc bag. Lay the bag flat on the counter or table and gently push out any excess air. Fasten the end of the Ziploc bag. Place a piece of tape over the opening to ensure the squishy mixture does not escape. Tape the squishy bag onto the counter or table. Now let your preschooler draw letters, shapes, and numbers.

LOW PREP *Say It, Trace It, Write It Uppercase Letters*

Materials:

☐ Say It, Trace It, Write It Uppercase Letters Activity Page (Appendix AM)
☐ Pencil

Directions:

Ask your preschooler if he would like to practice writing his letters. Show him the *Say It, Trace It, Write It Uppercase Letters* activity page. Explain to him he will first tell you the letter. Next, he will trace the dotted uppercase letter. Finally, he will practice writing the uppercase letter himself.

As a child I was taught that when learning to write, you MUST start with your pencil at the top of the line and go down to the bottom. Some teachers are still very adamant that students must learn to write this way, claiming it makes writing faster and more legible. However, other teachers allow students to choose if they want to form letters and numbers from the top or bottom, either is considered acceptable as long as the student's writing is legible. You are the best judge for your child.

With my oldest, I taught him to form letters and numbers at the top since that is how I learned, but as my second child was starting to write I noticed he formed a lot of his letters by starting at the bottom. What is best for one child may not be what is best for another. For some children, it is easier to start at the bottom and for others it is easier to start at the top. The focus should be on fluid motion and readability of the writing.

——————————— ★ ———————————

LOW PREP *Say It, Trace It, Write It Lowercase Letters*

Materials:

☐ Say It, Trace It, Write It Lowercase Letters Activity Page (Appendix AN)
☐ Pencil

Directions:

Ask your preschooler if he would like to practice writing his letters. Show him the *Say It, Trace It, Write It Lowercase Letters* activity page. Explain to him that he will first tell you the letter. Next, he will trace the dotted lowercase letter. Finally, he will practice writing the lowercase letter himself. This is a lot of writing to practice at one time, so feel free to break this activity up throughout the day or utilize multiple days.

LOW PREP I Can Write My Name

Materials:

- ☐ Paper
- ☐ Crayon
- ☐ Pencil
- ☐ Marker
- ☐ Pen
- ☐ Colored Pencil
- ☐ Paintbrush

Directions:

If your preschooler has been practicing writing his letters, encourage him to practice writing his name using upper and lowercase letters. You can make dotted letters for him to trace or he can practice forming the letters himself. If your preschooler is new to writing, make dotted uppercase letters of his name for him to trace.

Show your preschooler each writing tool (crayon, pencil, pen, marker, etc.) he can choose from to write his name. Ask him to pick a writing tool and use it to trace or write his name on the piece of paper. Next, encourage him to select another writing tool to write his name. Let him continue practicing writing his name until he wants to do something else.

★

LOW PREP Rainbow Writing

Materials:

- ☐ Rainbow Writing Activity Page (Appendix AO)
- ☐ Crayons
- ☐ Dice

Directions:

Ask your preschooler if he would like to turn words into rainbows. Show your preschooler the *Rainbow Writing* activity page. Ask him to choose a word to write on the lines. (It is always a good idea to encourage him to practice writing his name.) If your preschooler is a skilled writer, use upper and lowercase letters; but if your preschooler is still new to writing, please use only uppercase letters.

Explain to your preschooler that he will roll the dice. Ask him to count the dots on the dice. He will look on the activity page to see what color crayon he will need to use to trace his name. If he rolls a one, he will use a red crayon. Two is orange. Three is yellow. Four is green. Five is blue. Six is purple. After he traces his name, let him roll the dice again to see what color crayon he will use for the second tracing of his name. Repeat this process several times. He will trace over his name each time to form a rainbow of colors.

LOW PREP Draw a Map of Your Bedroom and Label It

Materials:

☐ Paper   ☐ Pencil   ☐ Crayons

Directions:

Ask your preschooler if he would enjoy drawing a map of his bedroom. You can choose to draw a map of your house, his bedroom, or your neighborhood. It is a good idea to start with just a single room, and then progress to more difficult maps.

Place a piece of paper in front of your preschooler. Ask him to draw a big square on the piece of paper (if his room is a different shape, ask him to draw that shape on his paper). Now ask him to draw the objects that are in his room: a door, bed, closet, shelf, dresser, toys, etc. When he has finished drawing each object in the correct place, ask him to label each object. You may help him spell the words, or if he is good at sounding out letters, ask him to sound out the words to spell them. After he labels each object in his room, let him color his map.

Let your preschooler share his map with another family member.

★

LOW PREP Write a Letter

Materials:

☐ Paper   ☐ Crayons   ☐ Stamp
☐ Pencil   ☐ Envelope

Directions:

Ask your preschooler if he would like to write a letter to his grandparents, friend, or a family member. If it is close to Christmas, it is always fun to write a letter to Santa as well. Place a piece of paper in front of your preschooler. Ask him to draw a picture of something fun he did the past week that he would like to share. After he draws and colors his picture, ask him to label the picture, or write a sentence telling what is happening in the picture. If needed, draw lines for him to write on, help with spelling, or even make dotted letters for him to trace.

Once he has completed his writing, address the envelope. Explain to your preschooler what is needed on the envelope so the mail carrier knows how to deliver the mail to the correct person. Ask your preschooler to place a stamp on the envelope. Walk with your preschooler to place the letter in the mailbox.

LOW PREP *Sentence Scramble*

Materials:

- ☐ Sentence Scramble Activity Page (Appendix AP)
- ☐ Pencil
- ☐ Crayons
- ☐ Scissors
- ☐ Glue

Directions:

Ask your preschooler if he would like to unscramble a sentence. Explain to him that a sentence became scrambled and you need help putting it in the right order. Show him the *Sentence Scramble* activity page. Ask him to cut out the pictures at the bottom of the page. After he cuts them out, read the words at the bottom of each picture. Ask your preschooler which word he thinks comes first in the sentence. Ask him to place the cut-out in the first box at the top of the activity page. Continue this until each box is filled. Now, read the sentence to him. If the sentence is correct, have him glue the pictures in place. If the sentence is incorrect, ask him if there are any changes he needs to make in order for the sentence to be correct.

After the pictures are glued down, ask your preschooler to write the sentence on the lines below the picture. Explain to him that when he writes a sentence, there are spaces between words to help the reader see each word clearly. An easy way to remind your preschooler to include the space between words is to ask him to place his index finger after the last letter of the word. The first letter of the new word will start to the right of his index finger.

⬛ LOW PREP ⬛ Antonym Acting

Directions:

Ask your preschooler if he would enjoy playing an acting game. Explain to him that he will be acting out antonyms. You will call out a word and it is his role to act out the antonym or opposite of that word. Explain to him that antonyms are two words with the opposite meaning. Give him an example by saying, "Day is the opposite of night, so these words are antonyms."

Ask your preschooler what is the antonym or opposite of sad. He should say happy. Ask him to act out happy. Here is a list of antonyms:

Sad/happy, tall/short, fast/slow, loud/quiet, up/down, stop/go, below/above, give/take, right/left, hot/cold, silly/serious, weak/strong, big/small, near/far, open/closed, short/long, big/little, boy/girl, full/empty, and clean/dirty.

★

Antonym Go Fish

Materials:

- ☐ Antonym Go Fish Activity Pages (Appendix AQ)
- ☐ Scissors

Directions:

Cut out each card on the *Antonym Go Fish* activity pages and shuffle them. Ask your preschooler if he would enjoy playing Go Fish. Explain to him you will each receive four cards. Place the extra cards in a stack between the two of you. He will look at his cards to see if he can match any antonym (opposite words). If he does not have any matches, when it is his turn, he will ask you for the antonym or opposite of one of the cards in his hand. If you do not have the card in your hand you can tell him "Go fish," and he will draw a card from the center pile. If he draws a match, he can lay it down to the side. Now, it is the next player's turn. The player with the most matches at the end wins!

For example, you and your preschooler will both have four cards in your hand. Let's pretend he has the cards: fast, stop, cold, and young. You have the cards: tall, awake, day, and old. When it is your preschooler's turn, he can ask you if you have the antonym of stop. Ask him to tell you the antonym of stop. He should say, "The antonym is go." You do not have the word "go", so he will need to draw a card from the center stack of cards. When he draws a card from the center stack, he might draw the word "go"; therefore, he will have a match and be able to lay it down next to him. Now it is your turn.

LOW PREP   Connect the Synonyms

Materials:

- ☐ Connect the Synonyms Activity Page (Appendix AR)
- ☐ Pencil

Directions:

Ask your preschooler if he would like to learn about synonyms today. Explain to him that synonyms are words that have the same meaning. Give him an example by saying, "A synonym for the word pretty, is the word beautiful." Tell him a trick to help him remember that synonyms are words with the same meaning by saying, "Synonym starts with the letter 'S' and the word same starts with the letter 'S.'"

Show your preschooler the *Connect the Synonyms* activity page. Explain that together you will read a word on the left-hand column. Next, you will read through the words on the right-hand column to find a word that has the same meaning. When you find the match, your preschooler will draw a line to connect the two synonyms.

★

Synonym Eggs

Materials:

- ☐ 6-10 Plastic Eggs
- ☐ Marker

Directions:

Prepare this activity by writing synonyms on each plastic egg half. For example, write "little" on the bottom half of the plastic egg and "tiny" on the top half of the plastic egg. These words are synonyms because they have the same meaning. Some other synonyms are: big/large, happy/glad, angry/mad, fast/quick, look/see, hear/listen, kind/nice, hop/jump, sick/ill, and bag/sack. After you write the synonym pairs on the eggs, break them apart. Keep the top halves grouped together and the bottom halves grouped together.

Ask your preschooler if he would enjoy playing a matching game. Show him the eggs. Explain to him he will pick a top egg half, read the word on the egg, and then he will need to find the synonym for the word from the bottom egg halves. Ask your preschooler to tell you the meaning of synonym. If needed, you can help him. Play the game until each synonym is matched correctly.

LOW PREP ## Color the Synonyms and Antonyms

Materials:

☐ Color the Synonyms and Antonyms Activity Page (Appendix AS)
☐ Crayons

Directions:

Ask your preschooler if he would like to color. Show him the *Color the Synonyms and Antonyms* activity page. Read the directions to him. He will color the antonyms red, and the synonyms green. Ask your preschooler if he can explain an antonym and synonym. You can clarify as needed.

Ask your child if he would like to color synonyms or antonyms first. If he decides to color antonyms first, color all antonyms before moving onto synonyms. Read each group of words and let your preschooler decide if it is an antonym or synonym. If it is an antonym, he can color it, but if it is a synonym leave it blank and move to the next apple. Continue until all antonyms are colored. Now ask your preschooler to color the synonyms. If your preschooler needs a break, please take one and complete the activity at a later time.

★

Homonym Puzzles

Materials:

☐ Homonym Puzzles Activity Pages (Appendix AT)
☐ Scissors

Directions:

Cut out the pieces from the *Homonym Puzzles* activity pages. Ask your preschooler if he knows that some words have two different meanings. Tell him that these words are called homonyms. Give him an example by saying, "The word 'bat' can mean a baseball bat or a flying animal. "

Show your preschooler the *Homonym Puzzles* pieces. Explain that he will pick a word from the pieces, and you will read it together. Next, he must find the two pictures that match the word. Do this until all the puzzles are complete.

LOW PREP *Draw Homonyms*

Materials:

- ☐ Homonyms Activity Page (Appendix AU)
- ☐ Pencil
- ☐ Crayons

Directions:

Ask your preschooler if he would enjoy drawing different homonyms. Ask him to tell you the meaning of a homonym. Show your preschooler the *Homonyms* activity page. Explain that together you will write a homonym in the top box, and then your preschooler will draw a picture of the two meanings in the boxes below the homonym.

For example, help your preschooler write the word "letter" in the homonym box. Next, ask him to draw a picture of a letter from the alphabet in one of the boxes below the word "letter." Finally, ask him to draw a picture of a letter that can be mailed.

Here are a few examples of homonyms: scale (a fish scale and weight scale), ring (a telephone ringing and a ring for your finger), palm (palm of a hand and palm tree), chest (treasure chest and human chest), and saw (tool saw and looking with your eyes).

LOW PREP Pick the Punctuation

Materials:

- ☐ Pick the Punctuation Activity Page (Appendix AV)
- ☐ Pencil

Directions:

Ask your preschooler if he would like to pick the punctuation that goes at the end of each sentence. Ask your preschooler if he knows what the word "punctuation" means. Explain to your preschooler there are marks placed at the end of each sentence to assist the reader in knowing how to read the sentence and to inform the reader the sentence has ended. It also allows the reader to take a breath before the next sentence.

Show your preschooler the *Pick the Punctuation* activity page. Show him the punctuation choices on the right-hand side of the page. Point to the period and explain that a period is used to make a statement. For example, "The cat is orange." Next, point to the question mark and explain that a question mark is used when you ask a question. For example, "How are you?" Finally, point to the exclamation point and explain that an exclamation point is used to say something exciting. For example, "I can't wait!"

Now help your preschooler read a sentence on the activity page. Ask him to pick the correct punctuation to end the sentence. He can circle the correct punctuation with his pencil. If needed, help him by re-reading each sentence, exaggerating the correct tone and expression.

LOW PREP *Punctuation Reading*

Materials:
☐ Paper
☐ Pencil

Directions:

Ask your preschooler if he would like to read the alphabet. Tell him you will be inserting punctuation marks in the alphabet. Review the definition of periods, question marks, and exclamation points. Explain to your preschooler that punctuation marks alter the manner we read. Punctuation marks can change the tone of our voice. Punctuation marks can cause us to increase the volume we use to read a statement. In fact, tell him the volume of his voice might increase or decrease depending on the type of sentence he is reading.

Tell him:

- When he sees a sentence with an exclamation point, his voice should increase in volume.

- When he sees a period, his voice might not change because the sentence is making a statement.

- When he sees a question mark, the tones used for the words in the sentence should change to reflect the fact a person is unsure or uncertain about some issue.

Give him examples of the manner punctuations marks alter the manner we read. For example, read the following sentences: "I'm so excited to see you!" raising your voice to show your excitement, or "Did you spill the milk?" lowering your voice to show concern.

Now write the alphabet on a piece of paper, inserting punctuation between the letters like this:

ABC. DEF? GHI. JKL! MNO? PQR. STU! VWX? YZ!

Once you have the alphabet written with the punctuation marks inserted, read the alphabet to your preschooler using expression and intonation (raising and lowering your voice). Ask your preschooler to copy you as you read each " alphabet sentence." Do this as many times as your preschooler finds enjoyable. Consider changing the punctuation each time.

▰ LOW PREP ▰ Air Punctuation

Directions:

Ask your preschooler if he would like to make air punctuations to end sentences. Explain to your preschooler that you will tell him a sentence, and then he will need to select the correct punctuation to "make in the air" to end the sentence. Tell him to hold up his hand like a stop sign for a period because it is the end of the sentence. Tell him to jump in the air when he needs to end a sentence with an exclamation point, because exclamation points show excitement. Tell him to make a thinking face when he would like to end a sentence with a question mark because questions make us think.

Say a simple sentence out loud to your preschooler. It might help your preschooler decide on the correct punctuation if you say the sentence with expression. Provide hints as needed. Here are some example sentences:

The dog is brown. (He should hold up a stop sign with his hand.)

What color is your shirt? (He should make a thinking face.)

I love you! (He should jump in the air.)

Wow, you did an awesome job! (He should jump in the air.)

Can you clean your toys? (He should make a thinking face.)

I need to go to the store. (He should hold up a stop sign.)

─────────────────── ───────────────────

▰ LOW PREP ▰ Correct the Sentence

Materials:

- ☐ Correct the Sentence Activity Page (Appendix AW)
- ☐ Scissors
- ☐ Glue

Directions:

Ask your preschooler if he would like to learn about capitalizing letters. Explain to him that every sentence must begin with a capital or uppercase letter. Show him the *Correct the Sentence* activity page. Point to the first letter in the first sentence and ask him if the letter is uppercase or lowercase. Explain to your preschooler that since it is the first letter of the sentence, he needs to correct it, and make it an uppercase letter. Ask him to cut out all the uppercase letters from the bottom of the activity page and place the correct uppercase letter at the beginning of each sentence. Once he has placed all of the uppercase letters in the correct place, ask him to glue them to the paper.

LOW PREP   *Read It, Fix It, Draw It*

Materials:

- ☐ Read It, Fix It, Draw It Activity Page (Appendix AX)
- ☐ Pencil
- ☐ Crayons

Directions:

Ask your preschooler if he would like to correct a sentence all by himself. Show him the *Read It, Fix It, Draw It* activity page. Explain to him that you and he will read the sentence together. Next, he needs to look at the sentence carefully and find a letter that needs to be capitalized or made into an uppercase letter. Ask him what letter should always be uppercase. When he finds the letter to change, ask him to circle it with a red crayon. Now, ask him to write the correct sentence on the lines provided. Remind him to place a space between words. When he finishes writing the sentence, ask him to draw a picture of what the sentence is about in the box provided.

SCIENCE

The National Education Standards are vague in describing "Science Standards" for a kindergartener. For this reason performance standards from various states (Florida, Texas, and Georgia) were reviewed to assist in developing this section. Science standards are written similarly to English language arts standards by building on key concepts from kindergarten to high school. The ultimate goal of science is to involve your child in formulating questions about the world around him, and engage him in investigating those questions, such as: why do the sun and moon disappear in the sky, how do plants grow, what is the difference between an animal and a rock, and will this object sink or float?

LOW PREP *Day and Night Sort*

Materials:

- ☐ Day and Night Sort Activity Page (Appendix AY)
- ☐ Scissors
- ☐ Glue
- ☐ Crayons

Directions:

Ask your preschooler if he would like to learn about day and night. Show him the *Day and Night Sort* activity page. Point to the pictures on the right-hand side and ask him if he would like to color them. Give him time to color the pictures. Now ask him to cut out each picture along the dotted lines.

After he has the pictures cut out, explain to him that there are activities he can do during the daytime, when the Sun is out, and activities he can do during the nighttime, when the Moon is out. Ask him if he can give you an example of an activity for day and an example activity for night. If needed, provide an example. Ask your preschooler to look at the cut-out pictures and decide if it is a daytime activity or nighttime activity. If it is a daytime activity, ask him to place it in the "Day" box, and if it is a nighttime activity, ask him to place it in the "Night" box. Once he has correctly chosen a box for each cut-out, ask him to glue them into the boxes.

Day and Night Craft

Materials:

- ☐ Paper Plate
- ☐ Paint
- ☐ Paintbrush
- ☐ Cotton Balls
- ☐ Yellow and White Paper
- ☐ Scissors
- ☐ Glue
- ☐ Star Stickers

Directions:

Ask your preschooler if he would like to make a day and night craft. Tell him he will turn a paper plate into a day and night time craft. Draw a line down the center of the plate. Ask your preschooler to paint one side of the plate dark blue and the other side, light blue. Allow the paint to dry.

While the plate is drying, instruct your child to draw a sun on yellow construction paper and a moon on white construction paper. Ask your preschooler to cut out each picture. Once the paint is dry, ask your preschooler to glue the sun onto the light blue side of the paper plate. Next, instruct your child to glue the moon on the dark blue side of the paper plate. Now he can stretch out the cotton balls to form clouds. Glue the clouds onto the light blue side of the paper plate. Lastly, your preschooler can stick star stickers on the dark blue side of the plate. Encourage your preschooler to find a place to hang his craft.

LOW PREP Oreo Phases of the Moon

Materials:

- ☐ Oreo Phases of the Moon Activity Page (Appendix AZ)
- ☐ Crayons
- ☐ Oreos

Directions:

Ask your preschooler if he would enjoy learning about the Moon. Show your preschooler the *Oreo Phases of the Moon* activity page. Explain to him that the Moon reflects light from the Sun which means it shows the light the Sun is shining onto the Moon. Tell your child the Moon also travels around the Earth. Since the Moon orbits around the Earth, the Sun is only able to shine light onto certain parts of the Moon. This is why the Moon appears to change shape each night.

Explain to your preschooler that he is going to make each phase of the Moon using Oreos. Start at the New Moon. Explain to him that the Moon is between the Earth and the Sun so the Sun is shining on the side of the Moon that is facing away from the Earth. In this alignment of Sun, Moon and Earth, it is easy to understand why we cannot see any light reflecting off the Moon. Ask your preschooler to open the Oreo and scrape off all of the icing to match the New Moon picture. Move counter clockwise from the New Moon explaining that the Moon's shape changes because of how much of the Sun's light hits the Moon. Your preschooler will open each Oreo and scrape off the icing to match the picture of each phase. As he is creating each phase, point to the phase of the Moon and tell him the name of the phase. When you progress to the Full Moon phase, tell your preschooler the entire face of the Moon shines because the Earth is in perfect alignment between the Moon and Sun. One might assume that in this alignment the Earth would block the Sun from shining on the Moon. However, the Sun is so much larger than the Earth, it does not block the Sun's rays from illuminating the face of the Moon. (The Earth has a diameter of approximately 7,918 miles and the Sun has a diameter of approximately 865,000 miles. Thus, the diameter of the Sun is 109 times greater than the Earth's diameter. Over 1 million Earths could be placed inside the Sun.)

After you complete this activity, you and your preschooler can check the Moon at night to determine the phase of the Moon.

Why Are There Craters on the Moon?

Materials:

- ☐ 4 Cups of Flour
- ☐ ½ Cup of Baby Oil
- ☐ Small Pebbles
- ☐ Round Cake Pan
- ☐ Bowl
- ☐ Spoon

Directions:

Ask your preschooler if he would enjoy making craters on the Moon. Explain to your preschooler that there are many rocks, meteorites, and asteroids that float around in space. The Earth has an atmosphere around it that protects us from the rocks in space but the Moon does not. Sometimes these rocks bump into the Moon and make craters. A crater is like a hole.

Ask your preschooler to help you mix together the flour and baby oil in a bowl. Pour the mixture into the round cake pan. Ask your preschooler to smooth it out the best he can. You might want to take the cake pan outside or put a towel underneath it. Place the cake pan on the ground and ask your preschooler to stand above it. Hand your preschooler some pebbles. Ask him to toss the pebbles into the "moon" one at a time. After he has tossed the pebbles into the "moon," ask him to gently pick the pebbles out of the pan to see what kind of mark is left in the "moon." Tell him this is the same thing that happens to the real Moon.

Make a Solar System Mobile

Materials:

- ☐ Planets Activity Page (Appendix BA)
- ☐ Crayons
- ☐ Scissors
- ☐ Hole Punch
- ☐ String
- ☐ Coat Hanger

Directions:

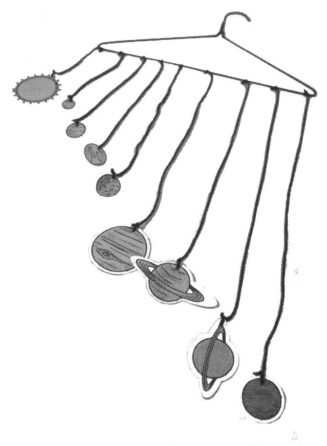

Ask your preschooler if he would like to make the solar system. Show him the *Planets* activity page. Ask him to color the sun and each planet. You may let him color each planet however he would like, or you can show him pictures of the actual planets so he can make them resemble the real planets. After he has finished coloring the planets, ask him to cut out each planet.

As he is cutting, cut the string to prepare to hang the planets. Cut nine pieces of string. Start by cutting an 8-inch piece of string, and then add 2 inches each time you cut a new piece of string. Therefore, you will need 8-inch, 10-inch, 12 inch, etc. pieces of string. This will help the planets hang without overlapping.

After your preschooler has cut out all the planets, let him punch a hole in each planet. Next, using the appropriate string, tie a knot through the hole of the planet. Tie the other side of the string onto the bottom wire of the coat hanger. Place the planets in this order: Sun, Mercury, Venus, Earth, Mars, Jupiter, Saturn, Uranus, Neptune.

Explain to your preschooler that all the planets revolve (spin) around the Sun. The ones closest to the Sun take a small amount of time to orbit around the Sun, but the planets that are far away take a very long time to travel all the way around the Sun. Neptune, the farthest planet, takes 164.79 years to travel around the Sun. The Earth takes 365 days, or one year to orbit around the Sun.

▰ LOW PREP ▰ *Settling Soil Experiment*

Materials:

- ☐ Soil
- ☐ Mason Jar with Lid
- ☐ Shovel
- ☐ Water

Directions:

Ask your preschooler if he would like to learn what is in dirt. Take your preschooler outside with the Mason jar and dig up enough soil to fill the Mason jar halfway. Go back inside and help your preschooler fill the jar with water. You want the jar filled almost to the top. Put the lid on the jar and tighten it. Ask your preschooler to shake the jar a lot. Next, place the jar on the table or counter and watch the soil begin to settle. As you watch the soil settle in the jar, discuss with your child where to find soil and how soil is used.

As the soil settles, it will begin to separate into layers. The finer pieces of soil, like clay and silt, will fall to the bottom while bigger pieces, like small rocks will be at the top. The small pieces of soil fall to the bottom because they are so small they can slide through all the openings between the rocks and bigger pieces of soil.

Your child will be ready to move to another activity before the soil completely settles in the jar. When he begins to lose interest, leave the jar and come back the next day to observe the manner the soil has separated into layers.

── ★ ──

▰ LOW PREP ▰ *Rock Washing and Sorting*

Materials:

- ☐ Rocks
- ☐ Bucket
- ☐ Water
- ☐ Soap
- ☐ Toothbrush

Directions:

Ask your preschooler if he would like to go outside to collect rocks. Go outside and collect a variety of rocks of different textures, colors, and sizes. Allow your preschooler to collect as many as his bucket will hold.

You will need to set up a washing station, either inside or outside. Fill a bucket with warm water and soap. Ask your preschooler to place the rocks in the bucket. He may use a toothbrush (toothbrush is not to be used to brush teeth after this activity) to scrub the dirt off the rocks he collected. Once he has cleaned his rocks, he can dry them off.

Now ask your preschooler to look at all of the rocks. Explain that he can sort the rocks into groups. He can sort them by colors, by the way they feel (rough or smooth), or by size.

LOW PREP *Exploring Volume*

Materials:

- ☐ Water
- ☐ Pitcher
- ☐ Variety of See-Through Containers in Different Sizes and Shapes
- ☐ Measuring Cup
- ☐ Funnel (Optional)
- ☐ Food Coloring (Optional)

Directions:

Ask your preschooler if he would enjoy playing with water. Explain to him that he will learn about volume by playing with water. Tell him volume is the amount of space an object or substance takes up or occupies.

Ask your preschooler to help you fill up a pitcher with water. Let him drop a few drops of food coloring into the water and stir it around. Place a variety of containers on the table in front of your preschooler. You can use a Tupperware container, water bottle, glass bowl, plastic cup, old dish soap container, etc. All the containers must be see-through. Now help your preschooler fill the measuring cup with one cup of water. Fill each container with one cup of water.

Ask your preschooler if one container has more water than the others. This is a trick question because all of the containers have one cup of water. Nevertheless, since water forms to the container it may appear as if there is differing amounts of water in the various containers. Ask your preschooler if one container has more volume (contains more water) than the others. (You are now asking the previous question in a different manner.)

Another way you can do this activity is to have your preschooler pour one cup of water into one of the see-through containers, and then pour the water from that container into another container. Continue this process for each container to see how the same cup of water changes shape to take up the space of each container.

LOW PREP Water Cycle in a Bottle

Materials:

- ☐ Plastic Water Bottle
- ☐ Blue Food Coloring
- ☐ Marker

Directions:

Ask your preschooler if he would like to see how the water cycle works. Explain to your preschooler that the Earth only has a certain amount of water. There is no new water; it goes through a cycle and is reused. Explain to him the Sun heats up the water and it leaves the lakes, streams, oceans, rivers, etc. and goes up into the air in the form of water vapor. When the water vapor hits cooler air, it changes back to water and forms a cloud. When the clouds get too heavy, the water falls back down to the ground as rain and goes into the oceans, rivers, streams, or the ground. The water cycle keeps going over and over again.

Ask your preschooler to draw clouds and a sun at the top of his water bottle. Next, ask him to draw water and land at the bottom of the water bottle. Now pour ¼ cup of water into the water bottle. Mix in the blue food coloring. Screw the top on the water bottle. Place the water bottle by a window that gets direct sunlight. Watch what happens throughout the day. You and your preschooler should be able to see the water at the bottom of the bottle start to evaporate and form water droplets on the sides and top of the water bottle. These droplets represent clouds. When the droplets get too heavy, just like the clouds, they will fall back down into the water.

LOW PREP *Hot Air, Cold Air*

Materials:

☐ 2 Flat Bottom Containers
☐ Hot Water
☐ Ice
☐ Cold Water
☐ Empty Soda or Water Bottle
☐ Balloon

Directions:

Ask your preschooler if he would like to see what happens to a balloon in cold water and hot water. Stretch the balloon over the opening of the soda bottle. Pour the hot (not boiling) water into one of your containers. Ask your preschooler to fill the other container with ice and let him pour the cold water over the ice.

Ask your preschooler to place the bottle into the hot water—he may need to hold it in place. Wait a few minutes and watch what happens. The balloon begins to expand and inflate. Now ask your preschooler to place the bottle into the ice-cold water and hold it. Wait a few minutes to see what happens. You should begin to see the balloon deflate. Repeat these steps as many times as he would like.

As your preschooler is moving the bottle from one container to the next, explain to him what is taking place inside the bottle. When he places the bottle in the hot water, the air inside the bottle is warmed. As the air warms, it expands and needs more space to move. Consequently, the balloon expands to make more space. When the bottle is placed in the cold water, the air is cooled and needs less space so the balloon deflates. The amount of air in the bottle remains the same the whole time, it just depends on how much space the air needs to move around as to what happens to the balloon.

Best Superhero Cape

Materials:

☐ Variety of Materials (Fleece, Cotton, Foil, Paper, Mesh, etc.)

☐ Scissors
☐ Safety Pins

Directions:

Ask your preschooler if he would like to test what materials make the best superhero cape. Together you can decide on a variety of materials to use. Gather items that are made from different materials so that your preschooler begins to understand the difference between plastic, glass, wood, metal, and cotton. You can gather things like aluminum foil, paper, a blanket, t-shirt, netting, towel, etc. To be precise with your experiment, it's best to cut all of the materials to be the same size and shape, but this is not necessary.

After you have gathered your cape materials, tell your preschooler you will use a safety pin to attach one material at a time to his shirt. Next, he will run 20 feet across the yard to see how well his cape flies. He will do this for each material. After testing all the capes, ask him which cape is the best superhero cape.

★

Sort Objects by Materials

Materials:

☐ Sort Objects by Materials Activity Page (Appendix BB)
☐ Variety of Objects from the Home (Plastic, Glass, Metal, Fabric, Paper, Wood)
☐ Bucket

Directions:

Within your home, collect a variety of objects for each of the six categories—wood, plastic, fabric, paper, glass, and metal. Items you might select include: shirt, pillow, blanket, lunch bag, notepad, mail, pencil, picture frame, blocks, yogurt container, glue bottle, dice, glass cup, jelly jar, Mason jar, pot, can, or fork. Once you have your items collected, cut out the signs from *Sort Objects by Materials* activity page. Lay the signs on the floor.

Ask your preschooler if he would like to play a game to determine "what things are made of." Explain that he will select an item from your bucket. Next, by using his sight, touch, hearing and ability to smell, he will decide what material the object is made of, whether it is made of wood, plastic, fabric, glass, metal or paper. Show your preschooler the example pictures on each sign as you are explaining each material. Finally ask him to place the object on the correct sign. Continue until all objects are sorted.

LOW PREP Candy Sink or Float

Materials:

- ☐ Candy Sink or Float Activity Page (Appendix BC)
- ☐ Bowl of Water
- ☐ 8 Pieces of Candy
- ☐ Pencil

Directions:

Ask your preschooler if he would enjoy discovering which kinds of candy will sink or float. Ask your preschooler to pick out eight pieces of candy, any size or type. Fill a bowl with water.

Ask your preschooler to write the name of the candy on the *Candy Sink or Float* activity page. Next, he will guess if the candy will sink or float before placing it in the water. Ask him to write his guess in the prediction column next to the name of the candy. He can write the words or just an "S" for sink and an "F" for float. Finally, he will unwrap the candy and place it in the water.

Wait a minute or two to observe the movement of the candy. Now ask your preschooler if the candy sank or floated. Have him write the results in the result column next to his prediction. Ask him if his prediction was correct. Do this for each piece of candy.

★

LOW PREP Objects Around the House Sink or Float

Materials:

- ☐ Various Objects from Around the House
- ☐ Bowl of Water

Directions:

Ask your preschooler if he would like to determine what objects will sink or float. Ask your preschooler to gather various objects from around the house to test. He can gather objects such as: marbles, Legos, toy car, ball, pencil, coins, bottle, spoon, dice, crayon, hammer, apple, etc.

Once your preschooler has gathered all the items he would like to test, fill a bowl with water. Ask him to select one of his objects. Ask him if he thinks it will sink or float. Let him place the object in the bowl of water to determine if he was right or wrong. Encourage him to test each object. As he is testing the objects, ask him why he thinks one object floats and one object sinks.

Inclined Races

Materials:

- ☐ Cardboard
- ☐ Scissors
- ☐ Books
- ☐ Toy Cars
- ☐ Tape

Directions:

Ask your preschooler if he would enjoy racing cars down ramps. Cut three equal tracks from the cardboard. Cut the tracks to be approximately 18 inches long by 4 inches wide. Now ask your preschooler to make three stacks of books, each stack at a different height. Place a track on each stack of books and tape the top edge of the track to the top book to prevent the track from moving.

Ask your preschooler to guess which track will make the car faster or which track will make the car travel further. Now ask your preschooler to place the cars on the stack of books. Push the cars down the ramp at the same time or one at a time. After the race is over ask your preschooler if his guesses were correct. Ask him why he thinks the race finished with the outcome that it did. As your preschooler continues to race the cars down the track, ask him to take notice of any change in the outcome of the race.

You can use the race tracks from this activity for the *Textured Races Activity*.

Textured Races

Materials:

- ☐ Race Tracks from *Inclined Races Activity*
- ☐ Books
- ☐ Paper Towel
- ☐ Aluminum Foil
- ☐ Tape
- ☐ Toy Cars

Directions:

Ask your preschooler if he would enjoy racing cars down different race tracks. Explain to him that you will wrap two of the race tracks in different materials to determine if it makes the cars go faster or slower. Ask your preschooler to help you wrap paper towels around one track and tape it in place. Do the same with the aluminum foil. The third race track will not be covered.

Ask your preschooler to help you make three stacks of books. All stacks should be the same height. Place the edge of the race track along each stack of books and tape it in place to prevent it from moving. Ask your preschooler which race track will be the slowest and which race track will be the fastest. Place the toy cars on the race tracks. Say, "1, 2, 3, Go!" Push all of the cars at the same time. Ask your preschooler which car finished first. Your preschooler should enjoy this activity numerous times.

Inertia Tower

Materials:

- ☐ Wooden Blocks
- ☐ Large Index Cards
- ☐ Hole Punch
- ☐ String

Directions:

Punch a hole in the center-side of ten large index cards. Cut ten 8-inch strings. Tie a string through the hole of the index card and then tie a knot in the other end of the string for gripping purposes.

Ask your preschooler if he would enjoy building a tower. Tell him that he is going to learn about inertia and Newton's First Law of Motion. Tell him Newton was a famous scientist who discovered three rules for science. His first rule states that an object in motion keeps moving unless a force stops it; and an object at rest will stay still unless something moves it. Explain to your preschooler that inertia is a resistance to a change in motion.

The object of our activity is to build a tower using blocks and notecards. After the tower is built, your preschooler will attempt to pull out the notecards, one at a time, without causing the tower to tumble. The blocks want to resist the change in motion (inertia). Consequently, they will not stay in place unless the card is removed quickly.

Ask your preschooler to place a wooden block on the ground, then a notecard (with the string facing him), then a block and then a notecard. Continue this sequence until your preschooler has built a tower to the height he desires. Now he will try to quickly pull out the notecard between the blocks using just the string. Tell him he needs to pull the notecard quickly to keep the tower standing. Suggest starting with the note cards at the top. Do this as many times as he would like.

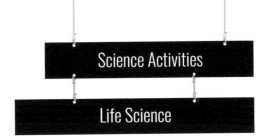
LOW PREP *Goldfish vs. Goldfish Cracker*

Materials:

- ☐ Goldfish vs. Goldfish Cracker Activity Page (Appendix BD)
- ☐ Goldfish Crackers
- ☐ Goldfish
- ☐ Pencil

Directions:

Ask your preschooler if he would like to compare a goldfish cracker to a goldfish animal. Explain to your preschooler that he will be learning about things that are living and things that are not living. Tell him that to be living, something must grow, breathe air, make babies (reproduce/ make more of itself), move, and need food and water. Tell him that he is living because he moves, he breathes, he grows, and he eats food and drinks water. Tell him that a rock is not living because it does not move, it does not breathe air, it does not eat or drink, it does not grow, and it does not make more of itself.

For this activity you can: purchase a goldfish, YouTube a video of a goldfish, or go visit a pet store. Ask your preschooler to look at the live goldfish and ask him if it moves. Ask him to write "yes" in the goldfish column. Now ask him to look at the goldfish cracker and ask him if the goldfish cracker moves. Ask him to write "no" in the goldfish cracker column. Do this for each question.

Ask your preschooler to answer the question at the bottom of the chart as well. Finally, let him enjoy a snack of the nonliving goldfish.

───────── ★ ─────────

LOW PREP *Living vs. Nonliving Sort*

Materials:

- ☐ Living vs. Nonliving Sort Activity Page (Appendix BE)
- ☐ Scissors
- ☐ Glue
- ☐ Crayons

Directions:

Ask your preschooler if he would like to sort living and nonliving objects. Show him the *Living vs. Nonliving Sort* activity page. Let him color the pictures. Ask him to cut out each square under the chart. Remind your preschooler that a living object must breathe air, move, grow, make more of itself, and eat and drink. Ask him to select a picture, and then ask him if it is living or nonliving. Ask him to explain his answer. Finally, ask him to place the picture in the correct column. Do this for each picture. When he has all his pictures placed on the chart, he can glue them in place.

Investigating Vertebrates vs. Invertebrates

Materials:

- ☐ Playdough
- ☐ Pipe Cleaners
- ☐ Small Blocks

Directions:

Ask your preschooler if he would like to learn about vertebrates and invertebrates. Explain to him that a vertebrate refers to a life form that has a backbone. You can let him feel his or your spine. An invertebrate refers to a life form that does not have a backbone—for example, a worm. Tell your preschooler that he is going to use playdough to build an animal with a backbone and an animal without a backbone to understand how backbones are used.

Use the pipe cleaners to form a shape of an animal with a head, a flat back, and four legs. If needed, cut the pipe cleaner. Ask your preschooler to mold the playdough around the pipe cleaner to form an animal with a backbone. Now build the same size and shape animal without a backbone. Make sure both have flat backs for easy stacking.

Ask your preschooler to place a small block on the vertebrate (backbone) animal. Place a small block on the invertebrate (no backbone) animal. Continue this sequence until the invertebrate animal cannot support the weight. Ask your preschooler what happened. Explain to him that a backbone is used to support the weight of animals and helps make them stronger.

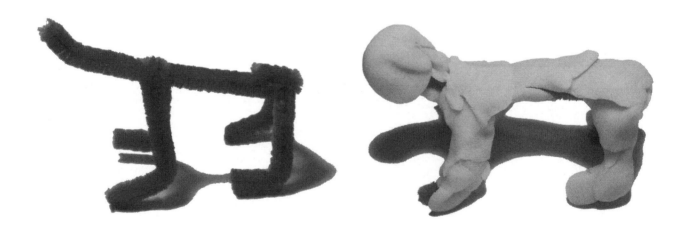

▶ LOW PREP ◀ Vertebrate vs. Invertebrate Sorting

Materials:

- ☐ Vertebrate vs. Invertebrate Sorting Activity Page (Appendix BF)
- ☐ Scissors
- ☐ Glue
- ☐ Crayons

Directions:

Ask your preschooler if he would like to group vertebrates and invertebrates. Ask your preschooler if he remembers the definition of the word "vertebrate." Ask him if he can tell you the definition of the word "invertebrate." If needed, help him with the definitions of the words. Show him the *Vertebrate vs. Invertebrate Sorting* activity page. Allow him the opportunity to color the pictures.

Ask your preschooler to cut out each picture. Ask him to choose a picture, and tell you if the animal he picked is a vertebrate or invertebrate (backbone or no backbone). Ask him to place it in the correct box. Do this for each picture. Once all of the pictures are sorted, he can glue the pictures in place.

Answer Key: Vertebrate - bunny, frog, bird, fish, and snake

Invertebrate - ant, octopus, spider, snail, and butterfly

LOW PREP Find the Mammal

Materials:

- ☐ Find the Mammal Activity Page (Appendix BG)
- ☐ Pencil
- ☐ Crayons

Directions:

Ask your preschooler if he would like to learn about mammals. Show him the *Find the Mammal* activity page. Tell him that you will read to him the top paragraph on the activity page three times to help him learn about mammals. Next, he will be asked several questions about mammals. Lastly, he will pick out pictures of mammals to color.

Read the short paragraph at the top of the activity page to your preschooler. Point to each word as you read it. Read it two more times. Reading the paragraph multiple times helps build retention and comprehension of the material. Now read the first question and the set of answer choices to your preschooler. Ask him to circle the correct answer. Praise him if he picks the correct answer. If he struggles with choosing the correct answer, go back to the paragraph and help him find the answer. This will teach him that it is a good idea to go back to the "reading material" to find the answer when he does not know it. Do the same for questions two, three, and four. On question five, ask your preschooler to pick out which animals are mammals based on what he learned. After selecting the mammals ask him to color them.

▶ LOW PREP ◀ *Measure Snakes*

Materials:
☐ Playdough
☐ Various Objects from Around the House

Directions:

Ask your preschooler if he would enjoy learning about reptiles and how to make a reptile. Explain to your preschooler that a snake is a reptile. Reptiles are a group of animals that have very similar features. Reptiles have scales. Reptiles are cold-blooded which means their body temperature changes depending on the temperature outside. Reptiles lay eggs. Reptiles are on their own after they are born. Explain that snakes are reptiles because they have all of the features just mentioned.

Ask your preschooler to select a color playdough. Show him how to take a ball of playdough and roll it against the table with the palm of his hand to make a snake. Make several snakes of varying lengths. Ask your preschooler to measure the length of each snake by using objects from around the house. You can use a shoe to measure the snakes. You can measure your snakes with: coins, goldfish crackers, crayons, pencils, etc. Have your preschooler lay the objects end to end beside each snake to measure the length of each snake.

For example, if your preschooler chooses to use goldfish crackers to measure his snakes, he will lay goldfish crackers beside one snake starting at the head of the snake and extending to the tail of the snake. Lay the goldfish crackers head to tail. Next, ask him what the length of the snake is using the goldfish measuring tool. Instruct him to count the goldfish. Do this for each snake to find the longest and shortest snake.

Life Cycle of a Frog Craft

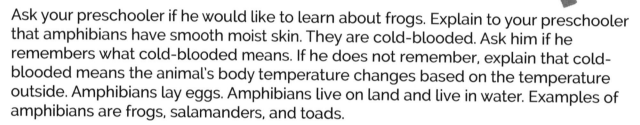

Materials:

☐ Life Cycle of a Frog Activity Page (Appendix BH)
☐ Crayons
☐ Scissors
☐ Glue
☐ Paper Plate
☐ Green, Red, and White Construction Paper

Directions:

Ask your preschooler if he would like to learn about frogs. Explain to your preschooler that amphibians have smooth moist skin. They are cold-blooded. Ask him if he remembers what cold-blooded means. If he does not remember, explain that cold-blooded means the animal's body temperature changes based on the temperature outside. Amphibians lay eggs. Amphibians live on land and live in water. Examples of amphibians are frogs, salamanders, and toads.

Ask your preschooler if he would enjoy making a frog. Show him the *Life Cycle of a Frog* activity page. Show him the picture of the egg grouping. Explain that frogs lay a lot of eggs at one time and the eggs are squishy. The baby frogs grow inside the eggs and eventually hatch from the eggs, but when they hatch, they come out looking like fish. Point to the tadpole picture. The baby frogs that look like fish are called tadpoles. As the tadpoles swim around and eat food they begin to grow legs and their tails gets shorter—point to the froglet picture. Tell your preschooler this stage is called a froglet. As the froglet continues to grow and get bigger, the tail disappears and the froglet becomes a frog—point to the frog picture. Explain that the new frog will eventually lay eggs and begin the cycle again.

Ask your preschooler to color the pictures and cut out the circle. After he has cut out the circle, he can begin to make a frog craft by coloring a paper plate green. While he is coloring the plate, cut out four strips (2 inches by 11 inches) of the green construction paper. Cut a half circle out of the green construction paper to be the frog's head. Also cut out a 1 inch by 6 inch red strip of construction paper. Cut two half ovals from the white construction paper. After your preschooler has colored the plate green, ask him to fold the green strips in paper accordion style. Now place two of the green strips at the bottom of the plate as legs for the frog. Place one strip on the right side of the plate and one on the left side of the plate as the frog's hands. Glue the strips in place. Glue the green half circle to the top of the plate to be the frog's head. Ask your preschooler to glue the two half ovals to the top of the frog's head to be the eyes. Draw dots on the white ovals, and a mouth for the frog. Ask your preschooler to roll the red strip of paper around a pencil. Glue the red strip of paper to the mouth—this is the frog's tongue. Finally, glue the life cycle picture on the center of the paper plate.

LOW PREP *How Fish Breathe Experiment*

Materials:

- ☐ 2 Cups
- ☐ Coffee Filter
- ☐ Rubber Band
- ☐ Water
- ☐ Coffee Grounds or Sand
- ☐ Spoon

Directions:

Ask your preschooler if he would like to learn about fish and how they breathe underwater. Tell your preschooler fish have moist skin and are covered in scales. They are cold-blooded. Ask him if he remembers what cold-blooded means, and explain if needed. Fish lay eggs. Fish breathe through their gills.

Ask your preschooler to place a coffee filter over the top of one cup. Wrap the rubber band around the coffee filter, so it stays in place. Now ask him to fill the other cup with water. Stir in coffee grounds or sand. Explain to your preschooler that the coffee filter is like a fish's gills. The cup of water with the coffee grounds is like water with oxygen. Ask your preschooler to pretend the coffee grounds are particles of oxygen in the water (normally you cannot see the oxygen in water). Now ask him to slowly pour the water over the coffee filter. Ask him what happens. Did the coffee grounds get caught on the coffee filter?

Explain that the water moves through the fish's gills and the gills filter the oxygen out of the water and send the oxygen to the rest of the fish's body.

Bird Beak Experiment

Materials:

- ☐ Tongs
- ☐ Tweezers
- ☐ Chopsticks
- ☐ Straw
- ☐ Pliers
- ☐ Cup of Juice
- ☐ Marshmallows
- ☐ Bowl of Gummies in Sugar
- ☐ Bowl of Rice
- ☐ Pistachios

Directions:

Ask your preschooler if he would like to pretend to be a bird. Explain to him that birds are a group of animals that have feathers. They are warm-blooded—remind your preschooler the definition of warm-blooded. Birds lay eggs. Birds have two legs and wings.

Explain to your preschooler that there are many types of birds and each type of bird has a different beak. Their beaks help determine what type of food they eat. Woodpeckers have strong beaks that allow them to peck holes in trees and grab bugs. The Kingfisher's long beak allows it to grab fish out of the water. The sharp beak of an Eagle helps it to eat fish and the skinny beak of the Hummingbird helps it to drink juice from flowers.

Lay all the beak tools (tongs, tweezers, chopsticks, straw, pliers) in front of your preschooler. Tell him he will use these tools to see what food is easier to grab. Place the bird food (cup of juice, marshmallows, bowl of gummies in sugar, bowl of rice, and pistachios) in front of your preschooler. Ask him to pick a beak and try to grab each type of food. Ask him which food was the easiest or most difficult to pick up. Do this for each beak tool.

LOW PREP *Animal Body Coverings*

Materials:

☐ Animal Body Coverings Activity Page (Appendix B1)
☐ Piece of Felt or Furry Fabric
☐ Piece of Mesh or Orange Sack
☐ Wax Paper
☐ Feather
☐ Scissors
☐ Glue
☐ Pencil
☐ Crayons

Directions:

Ask your preschooler if he would enjoy making different skins for animals. Show your preschooler the *Animal Body Coverings* activity page. Lay the felt, orange sack, wax paper, and feather in front of your preschooler. Explain to him that he will choose the type of body covering each animal group receives, based on what he has learned. He will glue the covering onto the "Animal Covering" box and then draw an example animal from the animal group.

For example, ask your preschooler about the type of covering he learned that mammals have when he completed the *Find the Mammal* activity. He should answer that mammals are covered in hair or fur. If needed, assist him with the answer. Ask him to find a material that is like hair or fur (the felt). Cut out a small piece of felt. Ask him to glue it in the "Animal Covering" box. Now ask your preschooler to draw a mammal in the "Example" box. Show him the *Find the Mammal* activity page to help him remember some examples. Do this for each animal group.

Answer Key: Mammals-hair or fur (felt or fur fabric), Reptiles-scales (orange sack), Amphibians-smooth skin (wax paper), Birds-feathers (feather), Fish-scales (orange sack)

Plant Seeds

Materials:

- ☐ Seeds
- ☐ Potting Soil
- ☐ Clear Cup, Planter, or Jar
- ☐ Water

Directions:

Ask your preschooler if he would enjoy planting seeds. If possible, take your preschooler to a gardening store and let him pick out the plant he would like to grow. He can pick flowers, vegetables, or fruit. Once he picks out seeds, you will need to purchase potting soil and a container to plant the seeds. (I used a clear cup for this activity so my son could see the changes that were happening each day.)

If your preschooler is patient enough, you can soak the seeds in water overnight to speed up the sprouting process but this is not necessary. Ask your preschooler to fill the clear cup half full with potting soil. Pack the soil. Next, ask him to place the seeds in the soil. Suggest placing the seeds close to the edge of the cup so he will be able to see the seeds' growth. Now, have your preschooler cover the seeds with potting soil. Pour some water over the soil. Be sure to avoid drowning the seeds. Place the planter by a window. Tell him that plants need dirt, sunlight, and water to be able to grow. Encourage your preschooler to watch the transformation each day.

As the seeds begin to grow into a plant, you can teach your preschooler about the parts of a plant. The roots help keep the plant in the dirt and soak up water and nutrients for the plant to grow. The stem carries water and nutrients from the roots to the other parts of the plant. The leaves take in the air and absorb light that is needed by the plant to make food and grow bigger. The flower or fruit produce seeds from which new plants are grown.

Once your seeds outgrow the cup, you can transfer the plant to a bigger planter or to the ground. As you are transferring the plant, be sure to show your preschooler the roots of the plant.

Plant Parts and Needs

Materials:

- ☐ Plant Parts and Needs Activity Page (Appendix BJ)
- ☐ Scissors
- ☐ Glue

Directions:

Ask your preschooler if he would like to learn about the parts of a plant and what a plant needs. Show him the *Plant Parts and Needs* activity page. Explain to him that "plant parts" are what a plant is made of and "plant needs" are what the plant needs to make food and live. Ask him to cut out all the words from the bottom of the activity page. Ask him to pick a word. Read the word with your child, and ask him if it is a "plant part" or "what a plant needs." Place the word in the correct box. Do this for each word. After all the words are in the correct box, ask him to glue the words in place.

What Effects Plant Growth

Materials:

☐ What Effects Plant Growth Activity Page (Appendix BK)
☐ 4-6 Plants (all the same)
☐ Potting Soil
☐ Water
☐ Salt Water
☐ Carbonated Water
☐ Soda
☐ Lemonade
☐ Juice
☐ 4-6 Clear Cups
☐ Ruler
☐ Tablespoon
☐ Pencil
☐ Marker

Directions:

Ask your preschooler if he would enjoy an experiment with plants. Explain to your preschooler he will be planting plants in cups. Each plant will be given a different type of liquid to see how it effects each plant's growth. Plant four to six plants for this experiment. Choose any type of liquids to apply to the plants, but make sure one of them is water. The plant, nourished with water, will be the control plant.

On the outside of each cup, write the name of the liquid you will use to nourish that plant. On the *What Effects Plant Growth* activity page, in the column on the far left hand side, write the name of each liquid you are using in the experiment.

Help your preschooler plant the plants in clear cups. To measure the impact of the differing liquids on plant growth, it is better to use established plants rather than seeds. After the plants are planted, ask your preschooler to use the ruler and measure the height of each plant. Write the height of each plant in the Day 1 column, next to the correct liquids on the *What Effects Plant Growth* activity page. Ask your preschooler to add three tablespoons of the specified liquid to each cup. (The amount of liquid added may vary depending on the size of cup you are using.) Make sure the correct liquid is being added to each cup.

On Day 2, your preschooler will measure the height of each plant and record it on the chart. Next, he will add three tablespoons of the appropriate liquid to each cup. He will repeat this process for seven days. As he is completing the experiment, ask him questions about what he is noticing.

SOCIAL STUDIES

The National Education Standards integrates history and social studies standards into the reading standards. For that reason, additional state performance standards (Massachusetts, Texas, Vermont, Georgia, California, and Florida) were utilized in the development of the following activities. These activities will acquaint your child with some of the foundations of American history, basic concepts of geography, and basic economics.

National Holidays

Please see section "A Gift for You" on page xiii.

Learning about National Holidays is a part of the Common Core Standards. In my book *The Ultimate Toddler Activity Guide*, I have a section on Holidays, which should be extremely helpful to you and your preschooler in learning about, and appreciating these special days. As a gift to you, and in appreciation of your patronage, I am providing you with a link, enabling you to access these activities. This link will give you access to 50 activities which will help your child learn about and celebrate: New Year's Day, Martin Luther King Jr. Day, Valentine's Day, Presidents' Day, St. Patrick's Day, Easter, Earth Day, 4th of July, Columbus Day, Halloween, Veterans Day, Thanksgiving, and Christmas. Here is the link:

www.bestmomideas.com/ultimate-kindergarten-prep-printouts

Password: bestmomideas4k2n

LOW PREP *Color the American Flag*

Materials:

☐ Color the American Flag Activity Page (Appendix BL)
☐ Red and Blue Crayon

Directions:

Ask your preschooler if he would like to learn about the American flag. Show him the *Color the American Flag* activity page. Read the facts about the flag to him. Point to each word as you read it, encouraging him to follow along. It helps with comprehension skills if you read the material to your child three times. Ask him questions about the reading. Finally, ask him to color the flag in a manner which matches the actual American flag.

LOW PREP *American Flag Fortune Teller*

Materials:

☐ American Flag Fortune Teller Activity Page (Appendix BM)
☐ Scissors

Directions:

Ask your preschooler if he would like to make a fortune teller. Tell him the fortune teller doesn't really tell his fortune. It's just a fun activity to make a paper American flag. Cut out the big square from the *American Flag Fortune Teller* activity page. Guide your preschooler through the steps of folding the fortune teller. Place the fortune teller in front of your preschooler so the corner with the stars is in the top left-hand corner. Ask your preschooler to fold over the four corners evenly, to meet in the middle. Crease each fold. It should make a smaller square.

Flip the square over. Your preschooler should fold the four corners evenly to meet in the middle again. It will make an even smaller square. Now, he is going to fold the right edge over to meet the left edge, make a crease, and unfold it. Fold the top edge down to meet the bottom edge, make a crease, and leave it folded. At this point, you should see the stars and stripes pattern on the outside of the fortune teller.

Ask your preschooler to slide his thumb and index finger of each hand, under the stars and stripes flaps. Push the edges to the center and it should make an American flag. Teach your preschooler how to push and pull his fingers together to make the fortune teller move. He will see questions at the center of the fortune teller. He can ask those questions and then lift the corresponding flap to reveal the answer.

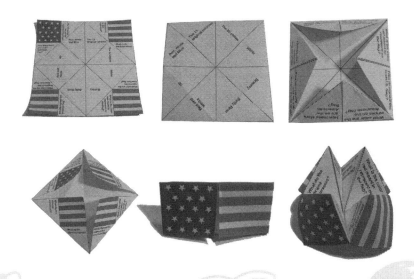

◄ LOW PREP ► *Fill in the Blank Pledge of Allegiance*

Materials:

☐ Pledge of Allegiance Activity Page (Appendix BN)
☐ Scissors
☐ Glue

Directions:

Ask your preschooler if he would like to learn the Pledge of Allegiance. Tell your preschooler the following historical facts about the pledge. Francis Bellamy wrote the Pledge of Allegiance for a magazine in 1892 to celebrate the 400th anniversary of America's discovery. In 1942 Congress passed an act making it the official pledge of the United States.

Some children say the Pledge of Allegiance in school each morning. Tell your preschooler that when he says the pledge, he should stand and face the flag and place his right hand over his heart. Now, practice saying the pledge with your child.

Show your preschooler the *Pledge of Allegiance* activity page. Explain to him that a few words are missing from the pledge and he will need to fill them in by cutting out the words and gluing them in the correct spot. Ask your preschooler to cut out the words along the right-hand side of the activity page. Now point to each word as you read it to him. When you come to a blank, ask your preschooler if he knows what word goes in the blank. If he does not know, say the word and ask him to find it from the cut-out words. Glue the word in place. Do this for each blank.

After he fills in the blanks with the correct word, read the Pledge of Allegiance to your preschooler again. This time explain what the words of the pledge are telling us. "I pledge allegiance to the flag," means I promise to be a good American. "Of the United States of America," tell us that even though there are 50 states we are one country. "And to the Republic for which it stands," means that every citizen gets to help decide the rules by voting. "One nation, under God, indivisible, with liberty and justice for all," means that our country can't be divided, everyone has freedom, and everyone must follow the rules of our country.

LOW PREP Star-Spangled Banner Word Search

Materials:

☐ Star Spangled Banner Word Search Activity Page (Appendix BO)
☐ Pencil

Directions:

Ask your preschooler if he would enjoy searching for words. Tell him that he will search for words from the Star-Spangled Banner. Tell him that the Star-Spangled Banner is our country's national anthem. As with the Pledge of Allegiance, everyone should stand and place their right hand over their hearts when they hear this song. If possible, find the song online and play it for your preschooler.

Provide a brief history to your preschooler about who wrote the national anthem. Francis Scott Key wrote the Star-Spangled Banner in 1814 during the War of 1812. The British had captured Washington D.C. and imprisoned some of its citizens. One of the men imprisoned was a friend of Francis. He was being held on a ship eight miles from Fort McHenry. Fort McHenry belonged to the United States and flew the American flag. When Francis arrived at the ship to talk to the British about letting his friend go, the Battle of Fort McHenry started. Francis watched the battle from the ship and saw that the American flag did not come down. If the British had won the battle, they would have replaced the American flag with their own flag. From Francis' experience of watching the battle, he wrote the poem that became the national anthem.

Show your preschooler the *Star-Spangled Banner Word* Search activity page. Tell him that the words at the bottom of the page are hidden in the letters at the top of the page. The words at the bottom are words from the Star-Spangled Banner. Ask your preschooler to find the word "banner." He will need to look for a "b" in the letters. When he finds a "b," ask him to place his finger on the "b" and see if an "a" is beside the "b." If it is, look for an "n" beside the "a." Continue in this manner as you attempt to spell the word, "banner." If there is not an "a" beside the "b," he will need to look for another "b." Continue this process until he has found each word. If he needs to take a break from this activity and finish it at a different time, please allow him to do so.

Make a Bald Eagle

Materials:

- ☐ Bald Eagle Template Activity Page (Appendix BP)
- ☐ Brown, White, Yellow, and Blue Construction Paper
- ☐ Scissors
- ☐ Marker
- ☐ Glue

Directions:

Ask your preschooler if he would like to make a bald eagle. Explain to him that the bald eagle was chosen to be an emblem of the United States of America because of its long life, strength, and beauty. The eagle represents freedom.

Cut out the patterns from the *Bald Eagle Template* activity page. Place the eagle's body on a brown piece of construction paper. Let your preschooler trace it and cut it out. Trace your preschooler's hands on the brown construction paper and cut those out. Place the eagle's head on a piece of white construction paper, trace it, and cut it out. Place the eagle's feet and beak on a piece of yellow construction paper, trace them, and cut them out.

Ask your preschooler to glue the eagle's body onto a piece of blue construction paper. Place the hands on either side of the eagle's body to be its wings. Glue the wings in place. Ask him to rub glue on the eagle's head and lay it above the eagle's body. Rub glue on the beak and place it in the center of the eagle's face. Rub glue on the eagle's feet and place them directly above the eagle's tail feathers. Now ask your preschooler to use a marker to draw eyes on the eagle. He can also draw lines on the tail feathers to create the appearance of different feathers. Finally, help him choose a place to proudly display his eagle.

LOW PREP *Statue of Liberty Dot-to-Dot*

Materials:

- ☐ Statue of Liberty Dot-to-Dot Activity Page (Appendix BQ)
- ☐ Pencil
- ☐ Crayons

Directions:

Ask your preschooler if he would enjoy learning about the Statue of Liberty. The Statue of Liberty sits on Liberty Island in New York Harbor. It is made of an iron frame and has sheets of copper hung over the frame. The statue is 151 feet and 1 inch tall. The Statue of Liberty was a gift from France and was dedicated on October 28, 1886. The statue represents freedom and liberty.

Show your preschooler the *Statue of Liberty Dot-to-Dot* activity page. Point to the tablet in the statue's hand and explain that the date July 4, 1776 is written on the tablet—this is the date America signed the Declaration of Independence. Ask your preschooler to find the number "one" on the activity page. Instruct him to draw a line from the "one dot" to the "two dot," to the "three dot." Continue this process until you reach the dot numbered "50."

LOW PREP Why is the Statue of Liberty Green?

Materials:

- ☐ Dull Pennies
- ☐ Vinegar
- ☐ Salt
- ☐ Water
- ☐ 2 Bowls
- ☐ Teaspoon
- ☐ Measuring Cup
- ☐ Spoon
- ☐ Paper Towels

Directions:

Ask your preschooler if he would like to see why the Statue of Liberty is green. Show your preschooler a bright cooper penny. Tell him the Statue of Liberty is made of bright cooper just like this penny, but the statue turned green. Ask him if he would like to learn why the Statue of Liberty turned green.

Ask your preschooler to fill two bowls with ¼ cup of vinegar and a teaspoon of salt in each. Stir the vinegar and salt together. Allow your preschooler to place five pennies in each bowl. Let the pennies sit in the bowls for one minute. Take the pennies out of one bowl, rinse them under water, and pat them dry with a paper towel. Now take the other pennies out of the bowl and just let them air dry on the paper towel. Do not rinse or pat them dry. The air-drying pennies will start turning green. Ask you preschooler to describe what he sees happening.

Explain to your preschooler that the green on the pennies is called a patina. This is what is on the Statue of Liberty too. It is due to the Statue of Liberty being exposed to the rain, snow, salt air, etc. As the Statue of Liberty air-dries, it starts to form the green patina that we see on the pennies.

★

LOW PREP American Symbols Book

Materials:

- ☐ American Symbols Book Activity Pages
- (Appendix BR)
- ☐ Crayons
- ☐ Scissors
- ☐ Stapler

Directions:

Ask your preschooler if he would like to make a book. Show him the *American Symbols Book* activity pages. Instruct him to cut each activity page along the dotted line to create the pages of his book. Stack the pages together. The "American Symbols" cover page needs to be on top. Use a stapler to staple the pages together along the left edge of the pages.

Read through the book with your preschooler. Read the facts on the page and ask him to color each American symbol. Do this until the book is complete.

Buy a Calendar

Materials:

☐ Calendar
☐ Pen

Directions:

Ask your preschooler if he would enjoy going to the store to pick out a calendar to buy. After returning home from the store, find a special place to hang the calendar that is easily accessible for your preschooler. Show your preschooler how there are different months. Read each month to him. Read the seven days of the week to him. With your preschooler, find family members' birthdays or special events to write on the calendar.

Turn to the current month and day on your calendar. Explain to him that each evening he will take a pencil or marker and cross off the day on the calendar. When he crosses off a day, ask him what tomorrow will be. This will help him start to understand the concept of months, days, and dates.

★

Clothespin Days of the Week

Materials:

☐ Poster
☐ Scissors
☐ Markers
☐ 7 Clothespins

Directions:

Using a different color marker for each day of the week, write the days of the week on each clothespin. One day per clothespin. Now cut a 14 inch by 3-inch piece of poster. Line your clothespins up in order (Sunday, Monday, Tuesday, Wednesday, Thursday, Friday, and Saturday). Starting at the top of the poster, color a 2 inch by 3 inch rectangle, using the same color you wrote the word Sunday. Directly under that rectangle, color another 2 inch by 3 inch rectangle in the same color you wrote the word Monday. Do this for each day of the week.

Ask your preschooler if he would enjoy learning the days of the week. Explain to him that he will need to match the day of the week to the correct color. When he picks up a clothespin, ask him what it says. If he needs help, read it to him. After he has the days of the week matched to the correct color, point to each clothespin, read it and ask him to repeat it. This is a great activity to do many times.

LOW PREP ✦ *Days of the Week*

Materials:

- ☐ Days of the Week Activity Page (Appendix BS)
- ☐ Pencil

Directions:

Ask your preschooler if he would like to learn the days of the week. Show your preschooler a calendar. Show him how the beginning of a new week always starts on a Sunday. After Sunday the days are: Monday, Tuesday, Wednesday, Thursday, Friday, and Saturday. Ask him what day will come after Saturday. Now show him the *Days of the Week* activity page. Explain that the days are listed in the center of the chart and he will have to decide what day yesterday was and what day tomorrow will be.

For example, show your preschooler that today is Sunday. Now have him look at the calendar and ask him what day comes before Sunday. You can direct him back to Saturday, if needed. Let him write the word Saturday in the "Yesterday" column next to Sunday. Now point your finger back to Sunday on the calendar. Ask your preschooler what will tomorrow be if today is Sunday. Slide your finger to the right to direct him to the correct answer. Now let him write the word Monday in the "Tomorrow" column next to Sunday. Do this for each of the days in the "Today" column.

▶ LOW PREP ◀ *Life Timeline*

Materials:

☐ Life Timeline Activity Page (Appendix BT)
☐ Pencil
☐ Crayons

Directions:

Ask your preschooler if he would enjoy making a timeline. Show him the *Life Timeline* activity page. Explain to him that some events happen in the past, which means something happened yesterday, a week ago, a month ago, or years ago. You can tell him he was born in the past because he was born __ years ago. Some events happen in the present, which means it is happening right now. For example, you are doing this activity in the present. Some events happen in the future, which means they have not happened, but they are going to happen. For example, Christmas will take place in the future. Feel free to name an event that took place in your preschooler's life and ask him if it happened in the past, present, or future.

Point to the "Past" box, and read the statement at the bottom to your preschooler. Let him fill in the blank of what he did as a baby. You or he may write his answer on the lines. He can then draw a picture of what he did as a baby. Do the same thing for "Now" and "Future."

▶ LOW PREP ◀ Now and Long Ago Sort

Materials:

☐ Now and Long Ago Sort Activity Page (Appendix BU)
☐ Scissors
☐ Glue

Directions:

Ask your preschooler if he would like to learn about items people used long ago. Explain to him that we didn't always have electricity, running water, cars, cell phones and many other things we enjoy today. Long ago, in the past, people used different types of inventions to travel to the store or contact a person. Before cars were invented, people used a horse and buggy to go to the store. Before we had light bulbs, people used candles to light a room. Before we had computers and email, people would often write letters to send someone a note. All of these things happened a long time ago, or in the past.

Show your preschooler the *Now and Long Ago Sort* activity page. Ask him to cut out each picture from the bottom of the activity page. When he is finished, ask him to pick up a picture. Ask him to name the picture. Next, ask him if we use the item today or if it was used a long time ago. Ask him to place it in the correct column. Continue until all pictures are sorted. Finally, instruct your preschooler to glue the pictures in place.

Land, Water, and Air

Materials:

- ☐ Land, Water, and Air Activity Page (Appendix BV)
- ☐ Scissors
- ☐ Blue, Green, and White Construction Paper
- ☐ Marker

Directions:

Cut out each picture on the *Land, Water, and Air* activity page. Now you will need to write "Land" on the green piece of construction paper, "Water" on the blue piece of construction paper, and "Air" on the white piece of construction paper.

Lay the blue, green, and white pieces of construction paper in front of your preschooler. Explain that the blue piece of paper represents water, and he will place things that live or travel in the water on the blue piece of paper. Ask him to name something he might see in the water. Tell him the green piece of paper represents land, and he will place pictures of things that live, grow, or travel on the land. Ask him to name an example of something he would find on the ground. Tell him the white piece of paper represents the air. He will place pictures of things he would see in the air on the white piece of paper. Ask him to tell you an example of something he would find in the air.

Now, place the pictures in front of him. Ask him to pick a picture. Ask him if he would find the picture in the water, on land, or in the air. When he decides, have him lay the picture on top of the correct colored construction paper. Do this until all the pictures are sorted.

◗ LOW PREP ◖ *Map Skills*

Materials:

☐ Map Skills Activity Page (Appendix BW)
☐ Crayons

Directions:

Ask your preschooler if he would enjoy learning about maps. Show him the *Map Skills* activity page. Explain to him that a map is a picture of a city, country, home, or neighborhood that shows us where things are located. Ask him to point to things he sees on the map. You can also show him things located on the map such as the streets and street names or the names of the different buildings.

Explain to him that you will read him one direction and he will need to follow that direction to be able to fill in the map correctly. This activity is great for building listening and recall skills. Read the first direction to your preschooler. Run your finger under each word as you read it, so he can follow along. It will help him recall directions if you ask him to repeat the direction back to you.

If he needs help finding Pig Street on the map, point to the word Pig in the direction and ask him to try to find the same word on the map.

▶ LOW PREP ◀ *Room Treasure Hunt*

Materials:

- ☐ Paper
- ☐ Pencil or Crayons
- ☐ A Special Object

Directions:

Ask your preschooler if he would like to go on a treasure hunt in his room. Explain that to go on the treasure hunt, he will first need to draw a map of his room. Tell him that to draw a map of his room, he is going to pretend that he is above his room looking down and he will draw a picture to show where everything is located. If needed, draw an example map of your living room to help demonstrate how to draw a map.

Place a piece of paper in front of your preschooler. Ask him to draw the shape of his room on the paper. Remember it will need to be a big shape so he can fit all of his belongings in the room. Now ask him where the door would go, where the window would go if the door is in that location, where the bed would go, etc.

Once he has his map drawn, hand him the special treasure object. Ask him to take the special treasure object to his room and hide it. He will need to remember where it is hidden. After he hides it, ask him to come back to his map and place an "X" on the map where the treasure is located in his room. Explain to him that you will take his map and use it to find the treasure. Go to his room and hunt for the treasure!

It's also a fun activity for you to draw a map, hide a treasure, and ask your preschooler to use the treasure map to find the hidden treasure!

Paper Mache Globes

Materials:

- ☐ Balloon
- ☐ Newspaper
- ☐ Flour
- ☐ Water
- ☐ Paper Bowl
- ☐ Paper Plate
- ☐ Plastic Cup
- ☐ Whisk
- ☐ Safety Pin
- ☐ Paint
- ☐ Paintbrush

Directions:

Ask your preschooler if he would like to make a globe. Explain to him that a globe is a round map of the Earth. Tell him that this activity will take a few days to complete, but it is a lot of fun.

First you will need to prep the area you plan to make the globe. This is a messy project so some precautions need to be taken to protect the area surrounding this activity. I recommend getting a disposable tablecloth to lay on the table and floor to help make the cleanup easier. (You can cut the tablecloth in half to use half on the table and half on the floor.) Now ask your preschooler to place a paper plate on the tablecloth, and then a cup, face up, on the paper plate. Now, blow up the balloon and tie it off. Try to make it as round as possible. Place the tie part of the balloon inside the cup. This makes a great stand for the globe.

You and your preschooler will need to tear a lot of 1 inch strips of newspaper. Now, make the paste for the paper mache. In a bowl, whisk together ½ cup of flour and 1 cup of water. You can make more, if needed. Show your preschooler how to place the newspaper strip in the paste.   Next, use two fingers to wipe off the excess paste so the balloon dries faster. Lay the newspaper strip across the balloon and smooth out any wrinkles. Now ask your preschooler to do the same thing until the entire balloon is covered. Let the balloon dry overnight. Repeat this process the next day. Again, let it dry overnight.

On the third day, ask your preschooler to paint his globe using blue and green paint. When he completes his masterpiece, it will need to dry overnight. Then you may pop the balloon using a safety pin to see the finished globe.

Where Do I Live? Book

Materials:

- ☐ Where Do I Live? Book Activity Pages (Appendix BX)
- ☐ Scissors
- ☐ Pencil
- ☐ Crayons
- ☐ Clipart Pictures
- ☐ Glue
- ☐ Stapler

Directions:

Ask your preschooler if he would like to make a book showing where he lives. Show him the *Where Do I Live? Book* activity pages. Ask him to cut out each circle on the activity page. Begin with the "My Home" circle and ask your preschooler to draw a picture of his home. Help him write his home address on the circle. Ask him to draw a picture of his neighborhood or street on the "My Street" circle.

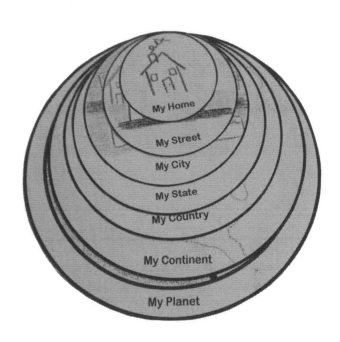

On the "My City" circle you can start to get creative with your preschooler by printing off pictures from things he would recognize around your city. Help him write the name of your city on the circle. On the "My State" circle you can print out a picture of the state you live in and ask your preschooler to glue it on the circle. Help him write the name of the state in the circle.

On the "My Country" circle you can print out a picture of the country you live in. Ask your preschooler to circle or color your state on the country map. Help him write the name of the country on the circle. On the "My Continent" circle, find a picture of the continent you live on and print it off. Ask him to glue it on the circle. Help him write the name of the continent on the circle. On the "My Planet" circle, show your preschooler the planet Earth and ask him to color it.

Place all of the circles in order from biggest to smallest, with biggest on the bottom. Staple the top edge of the circles together to form a book. Show your preschooler how the circle starts off small and gets bigger. Explain to him that his home is very small compared to the planet Earth. Each circle is a bigger part of where he lives.

◄ LOW PREP ► *Read a Book about Voting*

Materials:

☐ *One Vote, Two Votes, I Vote, You Vote* by Dr. Seuss

Directions:

You should be able to check *One Vote, Two Votes, I Vote, You Vote* out at your local library. If not, feel free to check out any children's book about voting. Ask your preschooler if he would like to read a book with you. Tell him that he will learn about voting and how the President is elected. Read the book together.

After you read the book together, discuss the following vocabulary words which he will learn more about as he does the government activities: President, vote, informed decision, ballot, and elect. Explain to your preschooler that the President is picked by the people of the United States to make decisions for our country. The word "vote" means a person is making a choice and picking that choice. Informed decision means you make a choice based on facts and information. A ballot is used by the person voting, to mark his voting decision and to submit his vote to the people collecting the votes. Elect means to choose or select someone by voting.

LOW PREP *Run for President*

Materials:

☐ Vote for Me Activity Page (Appendix BY)
☐ Crayons

Directions:

Ask your preschooler if he would like to run for President. Explain to him that the President is the leader of our country, the United States. He signs laws or rules of our country. He meets with leaders from other countries to try to solve problems. He also leads our armed forces or military. Explain to him that to be President of the United States, he must be at least 35 years old, born in the United States, and have lived in the United States for at least 14 years. Once the President is elected, he is the President for four years. After four years he can be picked again, or it is someone else's turn to be President.

Show your preschooler the *Vote for Me* activity page. Explain to him he will be pretending to run for President. Ask him what he would do if he was President. Ask him how he would help people. Ask him how he would spend the country's money. Ask him if there are any laws he would try to make as President. Now let him draw a picture of himself on the *Vote for Me* activity page.

★

LOW PREP *Register to Vote*

Materials:

☐ Voter Registration Activity Page (Appendix BZ)
☐ Crayons
☐ Pencil

Directions:

Explain to your preschooler that in order to vote in an election, he must first register to vote. Show him the *Voter Registration* activity page. Read each question to him and let him fill in the answers.

If he answered yes to each question, he can cut out the registration card at the bottom of the activity page. Ask him to draw a picture of himself in the portrait square. Ask him to write his name on the line. Help him write his address on the lines given. Tell him he is ready to vote in the next election.

Mock Election

Materials:

- ☐ Informed Decision Activity Page (Appendix CA)
- ☐ Ballot Activity Page (Appendix CB)
- ☐ Pencil
- ☐ Shoe Box
- ☐ Scissors

Directions:

Ask your preschooler if he would like to have a family election. As a family, you can have an election about choosing a fun activity to do together, a vacation to take, what to eat for dinner, what movie to watch, etc. Once you pick what your election will be about, come up with three choices that will be voted upon in the election. Show your preschooler the *Informed Decision* activity page. Explain to him that to make an informed choice in the election; he needs to think about the good and bad things about each of the three choices. In the boxes, above the smiley faces write each choice that will be voted on and draw a picture. Now ask your preschooler to look at the first choice, and think of why it would be good to vote for this choice. Ask him to write or draw his answer in the smiley face box. Now he needs to think of why it would be bad to vote for this choice and write or draw his reason in the frowny face box. Do this for each picture. This will help him make an informed decision about his vote.

For example, if your family decided to hold an election about what to eat for dinner. You would need to decide on three dinner items from which to choose. For example: tacos, spaghetti, and baked chicken. Using the *Informed Decision* activity page, you would help your preschooler write and draw the three choices in the top boxes. Each family member can fill out the activity page to help everyone make the best decision. After he draws his pictures of the three dinner choices, help him write or draw a picture of why each choice is good and why each choice is bad. For example, he might think tacos are a good choice because he likes the crunchy shell. He would write that reason in the smiley face box. However, he might think tacos are a bad choice because he doesn't like lettuce. He would write that reason in the frowny face box. Do this for each choice.

Once all family members have completed their *Informed Decision* activity page, ask everyone to review the pros and cons of each of the three choices. Tell them, in considering their choices, they must make a decision as to how they will vote. Make a ballot for each family member by using the *Ballot* activity page. At the top of the activity page write the name of the election, in this case "Family Dinner." Next, write the name of each choice on the lines given. You may draw a picture of the choices in the box to the right of each choice for those who are still learning to read. Show your preschooler and all other family members that they will put an "X" in the box next to their choice to cast their vote.

Cut a rectangle out of the top of a shoe box so everyone can place their ballot in the box when they complete their vote. Place the shoe box in a central location. Give family members their ballots and ask them to find a quiet place to vote. After each person has made his or her choice, ask each family member to fold his ballot in half and place the ballot in the shoe box. The next activity will allow you and your family members to learn the results of the election.

★

LOW PREP *Graph the Results*

Materials:

- ☐ Election Results Activity Page (Appendix CC)
- ☐ Pencil
- ☐ Crayons

Directions:

Ask your preschooler and family members to help you with the election results. Give each family member the *Election Results* activity page. Write the name of the election on the line at the top of the activity page. Help those who have questions. Write or draw a picture of the three choices being voted on in the tally boxes on the left-hand side.

Open the shoe box and pull out one ballot from the box. Open the ballot and read the result. Place a tally mark next to the elected choice on the tally chart. Show your preschooler and his other siblings how to draw a tally mark. Do this for each vote.

Now it is time to graph the results. First, family members will need to write or draw a picture of the three choices that were voted on in the bottom box of the columns of the graph. Next, each family member will look at the first tally chart choice and count how many tallies are in that box. Now, on the graph, color in the same number of boxes as tallies for that choice. Do this for each choice. After the results are graphed, ask your preschooler which choice had the most votes. The tallest bar graph declares the winner.

For example, if you were voting on what dinner the family would eat, you would write or draw the three choices in the tally chart: tacos, spaghetti, and baked chicken. Next, you would open the shoe box, pull out a ballot, and read the vote to your family. If the vote was for tacos, you would ask all family members to place a tally next to tacos. This process would continue until all results are read. Now each family member would write or draw a picture of tacos, spaghetti, and baked chicken, in the bottom boxes of the graph. Looking at their tally chart, each family member would count how many tallies are in the taco box. If the taco box had two tallies, everyone would color in two boxes above the taco picture on their graph. The winner is determined by which choice, taco, spaghetti, or baked chicken, had the most boxes colored in on the graph.

Community Helpers

Please see section entitled "A Gift for You" on page xiii.

My book entitled *The Ultimate Toddler Activity Guide* has a section on Community Helpers that will assist you in teaching your preschooler about some of the wonderful helpers we have in our community. The community helpers included are: dentist, doctor, fireman, police, and mailman. With each community helper mentioned, there are three unique hands-on activities. Here is a link to access those activities:

www.bestmomideas.com/ultimate-kindergarten-prep-printouts

Password: bestmomideas4k2n

LOW PREP *Goods and Services Sort*

Materials:

☐ Goods and Services Sort Activity Page (Appendix CD)
☐ Scissors
☐ Glue

Directions:

Ask your preschooler if he would enjoy learning about the difference between "goods" and "services." Ask him if he can explain the meaning of the words. Tell him "goods" are things that people grow or make to sell. Two examples would be shoes and doughnuts. "Services" are jobs that people do to help others. For example, the person who repairs your leaking roof or the person who delivers your birthday gift from Grandmother.

Show your preschooler the *Goods and Services Sort* activity page. Ask him to cut out all the pictures. Explain that he will pick a cut out and decide if it is a good or a service. Remind him of the meaning of goods and services. Ask your preschooler to place the picture in the correct box. Do this for each picture. After all the pictures are in the correct box ask him to glue them in place.

Answer Key: Goods: shirt, apple, scooter, car, shoes, and crayons.

Services: dentist, grocery store, gas station, teacher, pet shop, and chef.

LOW PREP ## Wants vs. Needs Sort

Materials:

☐ Construction Paper   ☐ Magazines   ☐ Glue
☐ Marker   ☐ Scissors

Directions:

Ask your preschooler if he would like to cut pictures out of magazines. Explain to him that he will be learning about "wants" and "needs." Tell him a "want" is something he would like to have for himself (e.g. a new bike). A "need" is something he must have to live (e.g. food and water). Ask him if he can name a few wants and needs.

Ask your preschooler to choose a piece of construction paper. Fold the piece of paper in half (hamburger style). Now unfold the paper. Draw a line on the crease that was created when you folded the paper. At the top of one side of the paper write "Wants" and at the top of the other side write "Needs." Ask your preschooler to look through the magazine and find some pictures that represent "needs." When he finds one, ask him to cut it out and glue it onto the "Needs" side of the chart. After he concludes this search, ask him to search for pictures that display his "wants." Once again, ask him to cut out these pictures and glue them on the "Wants" side of the chart.

★

LOW PREP ## People Work to Earn Money

Materials:

☐ People Work to Earn Money Activity Page (Appendix CE)   ☐ Glue   ☐ Crayons
☐ Scissors

Directions:

Show your preschooler the *People Work to Earn Money* activity page. Explain to him that people work to earn money to be able to buy things they need and want. Explain that parents work really hard, and are paid money. Parents spend the money on items the family needs like food to eat, a house to live in, and clothes to keep warm.

Ask your preschooler to cut out the pictures at the bottom of the activity page. Point to the first problem and ask him what he can do to earn money. If he does not say, "Work," guide him toward that answer. Ask him to glue the "work" cut-out on the first square. Point to the second problem and ask him what he will earn if he works. Ask him to glue the "earns money" cut-out on the square in problem two. Point to the third problem and ask him how he will spend the money he earns from his work. Ask your preschooler to glue the "buy needs" cut-out on the square in the third problem. Finally, ask him to color each picture.

Sort Coins and Dollars

Materials:

- ☐ 1, 5, 10, and 20 Dollar Bills
- ☐ Pennies, Nickels, Dimes, and Quarters
- ☐ Post-It Notes
- ☐ Marker

Directions:

Ask your preschooler if he would like to learn about money. Place the dollar bills and coins on the table for your preschooler to view. Play money works great as well. On a Post-It note write "1 cent," place it on the table and then place a penny on the Post-It note. Explain to your preschooler that a penny is worth one cent. Now write "$1" on another Post-It note, place it on the table and place a one-dollar bill on the Post-It note. Explain to him that one dollar is worth 100 pennies or 100 cents so it is worth more than a penny. Do this for the nickel and five-dollar bill and the dime and ten-dollar bill, as well. Now write "$20" on a Post-It note, place it on the table and lay a 20-dollar bill on the Post-It note.

Now ask your preschooler to pick a dollar bill or coin and place it in the correct group. Let him continue to sort the bills and coins until he would like to stop.

Next, show him how to make different groupings of coins to add to various sums. For example, you can write "20 cents" on a Post-It note and ask him to think of different coins that add up to 20 cents. Show him an example of grouping 20 pennies together. Help him discover how many ways he can use groupings of the different coins to total 20 cents.

Work for Money

Materials:

- ☐ Chore Chart Activity Page (Appendix CF)
- ☐ Stickers
- ☐ Pencil
- ☐ Small Treats
- ☐ Money
- ☐ Piggy Bank or Jar

Directions:

You will need to decide on a few age appropriate chores for your preschooler to complete throughout the week. Some age appropriate tasks include: cleaning up toys, feeding a pet, making the bed, setting the table, cleaning up the table, sorting laundry, fold towels, etc. Once you have decided, write those tasks on the *Chore Chart* activity page. Select whatever number of chores you believe are appropriate for your child. The chores you select do not have to be completed each day—for instance, laundry might only need to be sorted twice a week. Once you have decided on the type of chores and number of chores, you will need to determine how much each chore is worth if he completes it for the week. For instance, my oldest son's chore is to clean up his toys each night. If he completes the chore every night for the week, he earns a quarter on Saturday.

Once you decide on the amount of money your child will be able to earn, you can decide what type of items to buy for the "store" and how to price those items. Buy a few items that he might need or want. Examples include: markers, drawing pad, toy cars, trip to ice cream shop, new book, stickers, socks, cool toothbrush, etc. Price the items fairly—an item such as a marker should be priced lower than a trip to the ice cream shop. A trip to the ice cream shop should not be an unreachable price. However, price some items so he will to need to save his money for a few weeks to be able to buy the item. For example, my sons love toy cars and launching toy rockets with their dad so we have rocket engines priced at two quarters and toy cars priced at four quarters. Consequently, my sons must save for two weeks if they want a rocket engine or four weeks if they want a toy car.

Ask your preschooler if he would like to earn money. Tell him he will need to work to earn money. Show him the *Chore Chart* activity page. Explain to him you have written out a few chores he must complete each week. Read each chore to him. Tell him if he completes all of the chores each week, he will earn "X" amount of money. Tell him how much money each chore is worth for completing it. Tell him how much money he will lose from his weekly earnings if he does not complete a chore.

Tell your preschooler that after he completes the chore, he will get to place a sticker by that chore for the day. Explain to him that some of the chores might not have a sticker every day because it does not need to be done every day, but when you ask him to do it, then it must be done for him to earn a sticker. If at the end of the week he earns all of his stickers, he will receive payment for his work. He can then place his money in a jar or piggy bank. At the end of the week, he can go to the "store" you have set up, to decide if he would like to spend his money or save it for something bigger in the store.

Explain to your preschooler that to earn the sticker for the chore, you will ask him to complete the chore one time. If he becomes distracted, you will give him one more friendly warning to complete the chore, but after that warning he will lose his sticker for the day. This means he will lose the money for that chore for the week.

This is an activity that can continue to be done throughout childhood. It will help your child develop responsibility, gain appreciation for the value of money, learn to work hard, learn that there are consequences when a person chooses not to work, and learn the importance and value of saving money.

★

LOW PREP Create a Business

Materials:

☐ Business Activity Page (Appendix CG)
☐ Pencil
☐ Crayons

Directions:

Ask your preschooler if he would like to create a business. Show him the *Business* activity page. Ask him to think of something he would like to sell. Tell him it can be a good (something he makes or grows) or a service (something he does for other people). Once he decides on what he would like to sell, ask him to come up with a name for his business and write it on the line provided. Ask him to circle if he is selling a good or service. Now ask him to identify and write down customers who will be purchasing his services or goods. Finally, ask him to draw and color a picture of his business in the appropriate box on the activity page.

If your preschooler needs help writing his letters, draw dotted letters for him to trace. It is also helpful to write out the answers on a different piece of paper and let your preschooler refer to it as he writes his letters.

Play Grocery Store

Materials:

- [ ] Grocery List Activity Page (Appendix CH)
- [ ] Pencil
- [ ] Play Food
- [ ] Grocery Bags
- [ ] Money or Play Money
- [ ] Circle Label Stickers
- [ ] Marker
- [ ] Calculator

Directions:

Enlist the help of your preschooler as you gather together your food items and create your Grocery Store. If you do not have play food, use real food from your pantry and refrigerator. Write a price for each food item on a circle label sticker. Place the sticker on the food item. For example, bread priced at 75 cents, milk priced at $1, spaghetti noodles priced at 25 cents, yogurt priced at 25 cents, etc. Set your food items up along the edge of a table or in a "grocery store" you have created.

Hand your preschooler the *Grocery List* activity page. Explain to him he has a budget of "X" amount of dollars to spend on groceries this week. Explain to him how mommy and daddy are paid a certain amount of money each week. This money is used to pay for: the house, gas for the cars, food to eat, clothes to wear, etc. To ensure there is money to pay for everything, mommy and daddy must come up with a budget. Tell you preschooler there is a certain amount of money in the budget for groceries. Tell him that you must not spend more than the budgeted amount, otherwise there would not be enough money to pay for the other things the family needs. For that reason, he is only receiving "X" amount of money to spend on groceries.

Ask your preschooler to write his grocery budget amount at the top of his *Grocery List* activity page. Ask him to create a grocery list of food items he needs. Help him with letters as needed. When he has finished, he can walk through the grocery store. Ask him to write the price of each item on his list in the boxes provided next to the lines. If your preschooler wants to purchase a treat item, he can add it (and its price) to the bottom of his list. However, he will only be able to purchase it after he has bought all the needed items on his grocery list. This will help remind him of wants vs. needs.

After he has written down each price, help him use a calculator to total his grocery list cost. Start with the total budget and subtract each price from the total, or total up the prices and subtract that total from the budget amount. Let your preschooler help you push the buttons. If his grocery list stays within his allotted budget, he can begin shopping at the grocery store. If the total is more than the budget, ask him to make some adjustments. Unfortunately, on this shopping excursion, to stay within budget, he may need to remove his special treat item. Treat or not, he should have a very enjoyable shopping experience.

LIFE SKILLS

"Education Standards" do not address Life Skills. However, this is an important area that must be addressed. Although there are not specific standards for understanding these life skills, learning these life skills will aid your preschooler in developing independence and confidence as his kindergarten journey begins. Furthermore, his mastery of these skills will be greatly appreciated by his kindergarten teacher. These skills include: tying shoes, zipping and buttoning clothes, blowing his nose, and knowing parents' names, address, and phone number.

In this section there are also a few civil manner activities. These activities are a fun way to remind your preschooler of the values you have already taught him at home.

Fine and Gross Motor Skills

Please see section entitled "A Gift for You" on page xiii.

Fine motor skills are activities used to help your preschooler build the muscles and coordination in their fingers. Gross motor skills help your child build the coordination of all the muscles in his body. In my book *The Ultimate Toddler Activity Guide* there is a wonderful section with 17 activities to help your children develop their fine and gross motor skills. If you do not have my book, here is a link to enable you and your child to enjoy this section.

www.bestmomideas.com/ultimate-kindergarten-prep-printouts

Password: bestmomideas4k2n

★

LOW PREP ## Tie Shoes

Materials:

☐ Shoe with Shoelaces
☐ Pipe Cleaners

Directions:

Ask your preschooler if he would like to learn how to tie his shoes. Ask him to pick two pipe cleaners. The pipe cleaners can be the same color or different colors. Place a shoe in front of you. Take one end of a pipe cleaner and string it through the first hole of the shoe and tie it off so that it will not come lose. Do the same with the other pipe cleaner. A pipe cleaner should now be in the left and right holes of the shoe.

Pipe cleaners make learning to tie shoes easier because they keep the shape the child has made as he is learning how to manipulate his fingers around the laces during this process.

You may teach your preschooler using any tying method that you know, but here is a fun saying to help with each step:

Build a teepee (Stretch the laces up tall and cross them)

Come inside (Fold one lace over and through the loop)

Close it tight so we can hide (Pull it tight)

Over the mountain (Make a loop)

And around we go (Wrap the other lace around the loop)

Here's my arrow (Tuck the lace through the hole)

And here's my bow (Pull the loops tight)

LOW PREP *Zip and Button Clothes*

Materials:

☐ Clothes with Buttons and Zippers

Directions:

Ask your preschooler if he would like to master buttoning and zipping his clothes. Gather an assortment of clothes that include buttons and zippers. Clothes from all family members can add to the fun. Put all the clothes in a pile. Demonstrate how to button the buttons and zip the zippers.

Ask your preschooler to pick an article of clothing. Tell him to either button the buttons or zip the zippers. You may assist as needed. Now let him unbutton and unzip the clothing. When he starts to master the skill, you can turn it into a fun game by timing how quickly he can complete the task.

LOW PREP *Blow Cotton Balls*

Materials:

☐ Cotton Balls

Directions:

Explain to your preschooler that together you both will play a fun game about learning to blow your nose. Tell him he can use this skill to be a big boy and blow his nose in a tissue all by himself when he gets sick.

Sit side by side on one side of the table. Place a cotton ball in front of you and your preschooler. Show him you will keep your mouth closed and only blow out of your nose to move the cotton ball. The goal is to move the cotton ball across the table to the other side just by blowing with your nose. Demonstrate to him how he can press one nostril down and use the open side to blow. Next, switch nostrils and continue to blow the cotton ball across the table.

Race as many times as you would like. I do recommend cleaning the table after this activity to minimize the spreading of germs.

★

LOW PREP *Blow Bubbles in Water*

Materials:

☐ Bath tub

Directions:

Fill a bath tub with water to the appropriate level for your preschooler. Ask your preschooler if he would like to make bubbles. Explain to him he will make bubbles using his nose. Ask him to gently place his face over the water and submerge his nose under water. Ask him to blow out of his nose and into the water to make bubbles.

Magic Names

Materials:

- ☐ White Poster Board
- ☐ Scissors
- ☐ White Crayon
- ☐ Paint
- ☐ Paintbrush

Directions:

Cut a poster board into quarters. On one quarter of the poster board, use a white crayon to write your first and last name. Unless your child recognizes all his lowercase letters, write your name using all capital letters. On a second quartered piece of poster board, using a white crayon, write his daddy's first and last name. If you have water color paint, please use it for this activity. If not, you may use tempura paint and add a little bit of water to make it water color paint.

Explain to your preschooler that if he was ever separated from mommy or daddy, he would need to know your real names to be able to tell a policeman. This will help the policeman be able to get him back to mommy and daddy sooner. Tell him that you have hidden your and daddy's names on the poster board and he will need to paint over the poster board to discover the names.

Hand him one piece of poster board. Ask him to dip his paintbrush in the paint and begin to paint the poster board. When he uncovers the full name, ask him if he knows what it says. You can read it to him. Do the same for the other poster board. Hang the names up in a location he can see every day to help him learn your names quickly.

★

Make Your Own Color by Number

Materials:

- ☐ White Paper
- ☐ Pencil
- ☐ Crayons

Directions:

Write your name on a white piece of paper in block or bubble letters. Write your first and last name in all capital letters unless your preschooler is familiar with lowercase letters. Do the same for his daddy's first and last name on a separate piece of white paper. Now pick five colors of crayons. Write a "1, 2, 3, 4, or 5" in each letter. Now make a key at the bottom of one page. Write the number "1=" and the name of one of the five colors you chose. Do this for each of the five numbers and colors. Each number should have a different color.

Ask your preschooler if he would like to color by number. Show him the color by number pages you created. Ask him to read the names on the papers. Ask him whose names are written on the pages. Explain to him that he will need to follow the code at the bottom of the activity page to color the names. Read the code to him and explain that each time he sees the number one he will color it ____. Let him color your names.

★

Name Match

Materials:

- ☐ Poster Board
- ☐ Clothespins
- ☐ Marker

Directions:

Cut two 14-inch by 3-inch strips of poster board. Use the marker to write your first and last name across one strip. Be sure to leave a space between your first and last name. Write your name in all capital letters unless your preschooler is familiar with lowercase letters. Do the same for his daddy's name on the second strip of poster board. Now write the letters of each name on the clothespins. There should be one letter written on each clothespin.

Ask your preschooler if he would like to do a name match. Hand him one name strip. Ask him to read the name. Ask him whose name it is. Explain to him he will need to find the correct clothespin to place on each letter of the name. After he completes one name, ask him to read it again. Now he may work on the second name or save it for another day.

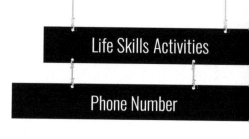

Phone Number Match Up

Materials:

☐ Paper   ☐ Marker   ☐ Index Cards

Directions:

Ask your preschooler if he would like to learn your phone number. The phone number he learns first should be the phone number you would write as his emergency contact. You will need to write the phone number on a piece of paper with dashes included. Next, write each number and dash on an index card, one number per card. Mix the cards up.

Ask your preschooler to look at the phone number on the piece of paper. Place your finger under the first number, say the number, and ask him to repeat it. Do this for each number in the phone number. Lay the index cards in front of your preschooler in random order. Ask him to put the phone number in order by following the phone number written on the paper. After he puts it in order, ask him to say the phone number to you.

★

Giant Phone

Materials:

☐ Paper Plates   ☐ Marker   ☐ Painter's Tape

Directions:

Ask your preschooler if he would like to dial your phone number. Using the painter's tape, tape the plates to the wall in a grid pattern similar to a phone keypad. On the top row of paper plates write numbers one through three. On the second row, write numbers four through six. On the third row write numbers seven through nine. On the fourth row draw a star, a zero, and a pound sign.

You may either write your phone number on a piece of paper or verbally tell your preschooler your phone number. Explain to him that as he hears each number, he will say the number and then tap the number on the wall.

You can also play this activity as a version of Simon by you tapping the first number in your phone number, and having him repeat your actions. Next, you tap the first and second number of your phone number, and he repeats your taps. Then you tap the first, second, and third numbers of your phone number, and he repeats you. Continue this for each number of your phone number. It's a good idea to say the numbers as you are tapping them to help with the memorization process.

Phone Number Stickers

Materials:

☐ Phone Number Stickers Activity Page (Appendix CI)
☐ Circle Label Stickers
☐ Pen

Directions:

Write each number of your phone number on circle label stickers four times. Show your preschooler the *Phone Number Stickers* activity page. Explain to him that you will write your phone number in the top circles. Ask him to recite each number of your phone number as you write it out. Or, you can say the numbers and he can repeat it to you. Next, ask him to place the numbered circle stickers in the correct order in the provided circles on the activity page. He will repeat the phone number four times.

★

LOW PREP Call You

Materials:

☐ Phone

Directions:

Ask your preschooler if he would like to use a phone to call you. Explain to him the etiquette of calling and answering the phone. Tell him when he is calling someone, and someone answers he needs to say, "Hello, my name is _____. May I speak to _____?" When he is answering a phone call, he needs to answer by saying, "Hello," or "Hello, this is _____." He needs to hold the phone close to his mouth so the person on the call can hear what he is saying. When the conversation is done, he needs to say "Good-bye," before hanging up.

I typically do not let my children use my phone unless we are calling or facetiming family. However, I do believe they should know how to operate a cell phone in case of an emergency. Please teach your preschooler how to open your phone and find the keypad to be able to dial a phone number. Once you have taught your preschooler how to operate the phone, let him use his daddy's phone to call you. Let him practice using his phone etiquette.

◀ LOW PREP ▶ *Make a House*

Materials:

- ☐ Paper Lunch Bag
- ☐ Tape
- ☐ Markers
- ☐ Index Card

1234 Silly Street
Funny, GA 56789

Directions:

Ask your preschooler if he would like to make a model of his house and learn his address. Tell him his address is where he lives. Place a paper lunch bag in front of your preschooler. Ask him to fold the top (where it opens) into a triangle by folding the two corners to meet in the middle. Tape the edges down. Now fold the bottom up so it resembles a house shape. Tape the bottom in place. Now flip the bag over. Your preschooler may decorate the house to look like his house. When he has finished decorating, help him write his address on the index card. Write the house number, street, city, state, and zip code. Point to each part of the address as you read it to him. Ask him to repeat it to you as you read it. Tape the address to the bottom of his house. Hang the house in a spot he will see it every day. Each day recite the address together.

───────── ★ ─────────

◀ LOW PREP ▶ *Trace Address and Rewrite It*

Materials:

- ☐ Paper
- ☐ Crayons

Directions:

Write your address at the top of a piece of paper. Place your finger under each part of the address as you read it to your preschooler. Ask him to repeat each part as you read it. Ask your preschooler to choose a crayon. He will use the crayon to trace over the address you have written. When he is finished, read the address together.

Now ask him to use another crayon or pencil to write the address under where you wrote it, by copying the address from the top of the page. Read the address together.

LOW PREP ▸ Address an Envelope

Materials:

- ☐ Envelope Activity Page (Appendix CJ)
- ☐ Pencil
- ☐ Crayons

Directions:

Show your preschooler the *Envelope* activity page. Explain to him he will write his address on the envelope and design a stamp for the envelope. You may verbally tell him the address as he writes it or you may write your address on a separate piece of paper and let him copy it. Let him write the address, and read it together three times before he designs his stamp.

★

LOW PREP ▸ Sequence Address

Materials:

- ☐ Index Cards
- ☐ Marker
- ☐ Paper

Directions:

On index cards, write your house number, street name, city, state, and zip code. Each part of the address should be on a separate card. Write your address on a piece of paper. Read the address to your preschooler. Ask him to repeat it as you say it.

Lay the jumbled index cards in front of your preschooler. Ask him to put the address in order. Ask him to tell you the house number. Ask him what follows the house number in an address. Continue by asking about each part of his address (street name, city, state, and zip code). If he is struggling to remember his address, allow him to look at the address on the piece of paper as a guide. After he completes the puzzle, congratulate him and ask him to recite it to you.

LOW PREP *Gratitude Game*

Materials:

☐ Bag of Skittles

Directions:

Tell your preschooler he has a lot for which to be grateful. Explain what it means to be grateful—being thankful for what you have in your life. Give him some examples of things for which you are grateful. Explain to him that you will open a bag of Skittles and you will each pick a colored Skittle. Each color of Skittle represents a different category for which to be thankful. Share each category with him:

Red-Name a person you are thankful for

Orange-Name a place you are thankful for

Yellow-Name an event you are thankful for

Green-Name a thing you are thankful for

Purple-Name something about yourself you are thankful for

Let your preschooler select a Skittle. According to the color of the Skittle, tell him the category of thankfulness he needs to think of and ask him to name what he is thankful for. Now you can take a turn.

★

LOW PREP *Dinner Time Thankfulness*

Directions:

This is an activity we do each night at dinner. We all love it because it helps remind us to be grateful for the little things throughout the day, even when we are tired, busy, or stressed. My children have even initiated the activity some nights.

Each night at dinner, ask each child what he is grateful for. You can explain that being grateful means he is thankful for the things he has or has done. You may start the activity by stating what you are grateful for that day. Ask each family member to participate.

LOW PREP *Toothpaste Respect*

Materials:

☐ Tube of Toothpaste
☐ Paper
☐ Marker

Directions:

Explain to your preschooler that he will learn about respect during this activity. Tell him respect is how you feel about someone and how you treat them. Explain that he should show respect to friends and adults, and treat them the way he would like to be treated—nicely.

Write the word respect on a piece of paper. Ask your preschooler to squirt the toothpaste over the word. After he has covered the word in toothpaste, ask him to try to scoop the toothpaste back into the tube. Give him some time to try.

Explain to your child that no matter how hard a person tries to put the toothpaste back in the tube, it cannot be done. Tell him it is the same way with our words. If we say something mean to someone, it often hurts his or her feelings. Even if you say you are sorry, you said something mean and you can't undo what you said. For this reason, you need to use respectful words. Give your child examples of respectful words (e.g. please, thank you, yes ma'am, no sir, no thank you).

Role play examples of respectful and disrespectful ways to speak to a friend or adult so your preschooler understands the difference between the two.

Responsibility Routines

Materials:

- ☐ Paper
- ☐ Markers
- ☐ Tape

Directions:

To help teach my preschooler about responsibility, I wrote down his bedtime routine steps on a piece of paper and taped it to his bathroom door. Instead of having to remind him of what he should be doing, he now refers to the chart. He has really enjoyed the responsibility of being in charge of his actions through this process. He has enjoyed it so much I also created a routine chart for our mornings. (Added Bonus: It is typically a smoother time because I'm not constantly redirecting.)

On a piece of paper write down your preschooler's bedtime routine steps. For example: 1. Brush your teeth. 2. Wash your face. 3. Go to the bathroom. 4. Put clothes in the hamper. 5. Put pajamas on. 6. Read a story. 7. Give hugs and kisses. 8. Get in bed. If your preschooler is not reading yet, draw or print out pictures beside each written step. Make the chart cute and fun! Tape the chart to his bedroom door or the bathroom door so he can reference it as he completes his nightly routine.

Show your preschooler the chart you created and where it is located. Explain to him he will be responsible for getting himself ready for bed. Tell him "responsible" means doing what you are supposed to do and accepting the results of your actions. Consequently, he will be in charge of looking at the chart to see what he needs to do next in order to get ready for bed. When he completes all of his steps, he can feel proud he was able to do it all by himself.

LOW PREP *True and False*

Materials:

☐ Index Cards
☐ Markers

Directions:

Ask your preschooler if he would like to play a game. Tell him it is a fun game that will help him discover the difference between telling the truth and telling a lie. Write the word "True" on one index card and the word "False" on another index card. Hand both cards to your preschooler.

Explain to him that you will make a statement and he will decide if it is true or false. If it is true, he will hold up the true card. If the statement is false, he will hold up the false card. Before you get started, explain to your preschooler what true and false mean. True means that the statement is real. The word false means that the statement is not real or true. Give him an example of a true statement. For example, "We live on planet Earth." Also tell him a false statement. For example, "The sky is purple." Point out that the false statement is false because the sky is actually blue.

Now play the game by making a statement. Make the statements fun. You can even let him make a few statements and you hold up the true and false cards.

At the end of the game discuss how it is always best to tell the truth, even when you have made a mistake.

★

Act of Kindness

Directions:

Ask your preschooler if he would like to do an act of kindness for someone. Explain to him that being kind means being thoughtful and nice to other people and not expecting anything in return. Share with him that it usually makes people happy when you do something nice for them. Some examples of acts of kindness are: do a sibling's chore, share a toy, bake a treat for a neighbor, write a thank you note to someone, hold the door for someone, leave a nice note for the mailman, take a treat to firemen or policemen, donate old toys, donate your allowance, do an extra chore, etc. Give your preschooler a list of three acts of kindness, and let him pick the act of kindness he wants to do. Now, ask him to complete the act of kindness.

LOW PREP **Marshmallow Test for Self-Control**

Materials:

- ☐ Big Marshmallows
- ☐ Plate
- ☐ Timer

Directions:

Explain to your preschooler that you bought him some big puffy marshmallows for him to enjoy. Place a marshmallow on a plate in front of him. Explain to him he can have the marshmallow that is on the plate now OR he can wait five minutes without eating that marshmallow and you will then give him TWO marshmallows to eat! Let him sit with the marshmallow while you step away and set the timer. Do not say anything to him during the five minutes.

When the timer ends, reward your preschooler with another marshmallow if he did not eat the marshmallow on the plate. However, if he did eat the marshmallow during the five minutes, simply say I know it was difficult to wait, but you only get to have that one marshmallow.

Share with your preschooler that the activity was about learning self-control. Self-control is being able to resist things he enjoys immediately so he can achieve bigger goals, like getting two marshmallows instead of one.

Self-control also means not acting immediately and thinking through decisions. For instance, if someone takes his toy, he might want to snatch it back right away, but having self-control means he will stop, think, and try to make the right choice. So, in this example, in demonstrating self-control, he would stop, think, and respectfully ask for the toy instead of snatching it back.

APPENDIX

To access printable, colored copies of the Appendix, please visit:

bestmomideas.com/ultimate-kindergarten-prep-printouts

Password: bestmomideas4k2n

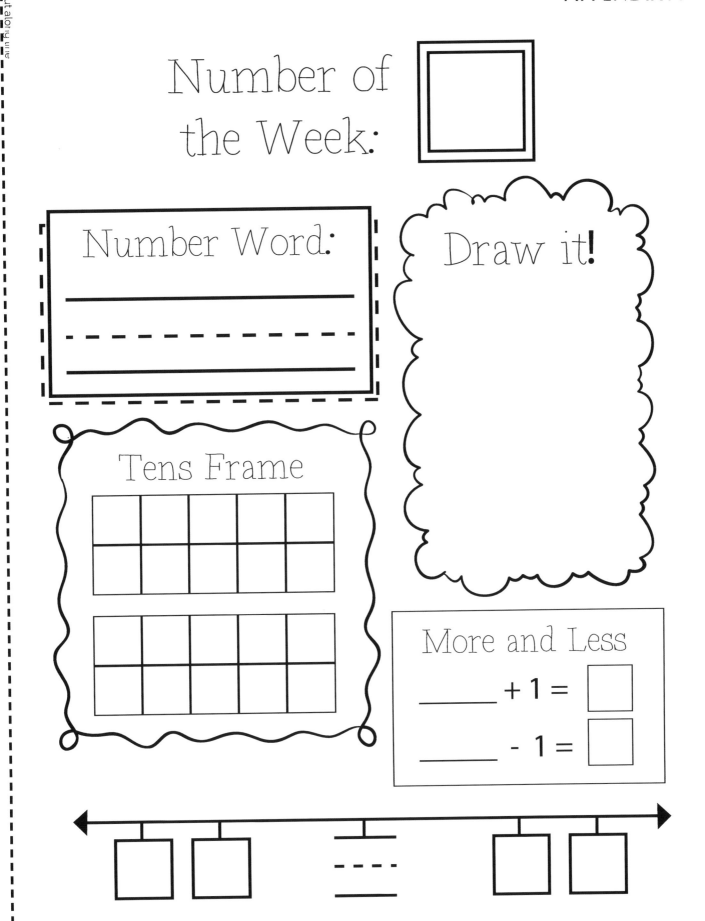

Number of
the Week:

Number Word:

_____

- - - - - - - - -

_____

Draw it!

Tens Frame

More and Less

_____ + 1 = ☐

_____ - 1 = ☐

cut along line

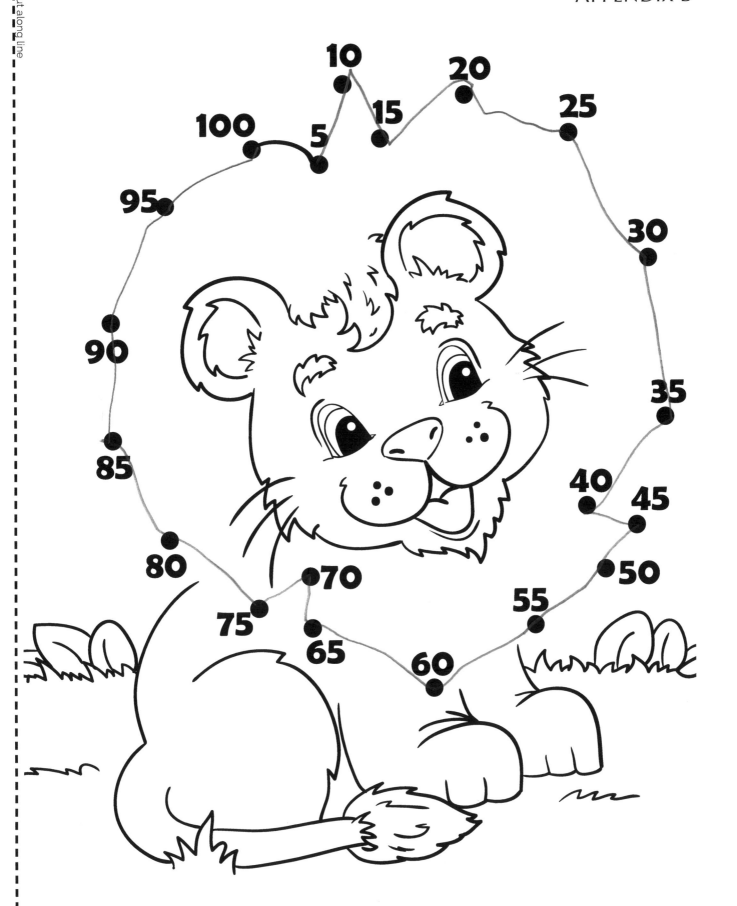

Sticker Number Line

Counting Forward

13, _____ , _____ , _____ , _____

22, _____ , _____ , _____ , _____

39, _____ , _____ , _____ , _____

51, _____ , _____ , _____ , _____

67, _____ , _____ , _____ , _____

75, _____ , _____ , _____ , _____

84, _____ , _____ , _____ , _____

90, _____ , _____ , _____ , _____

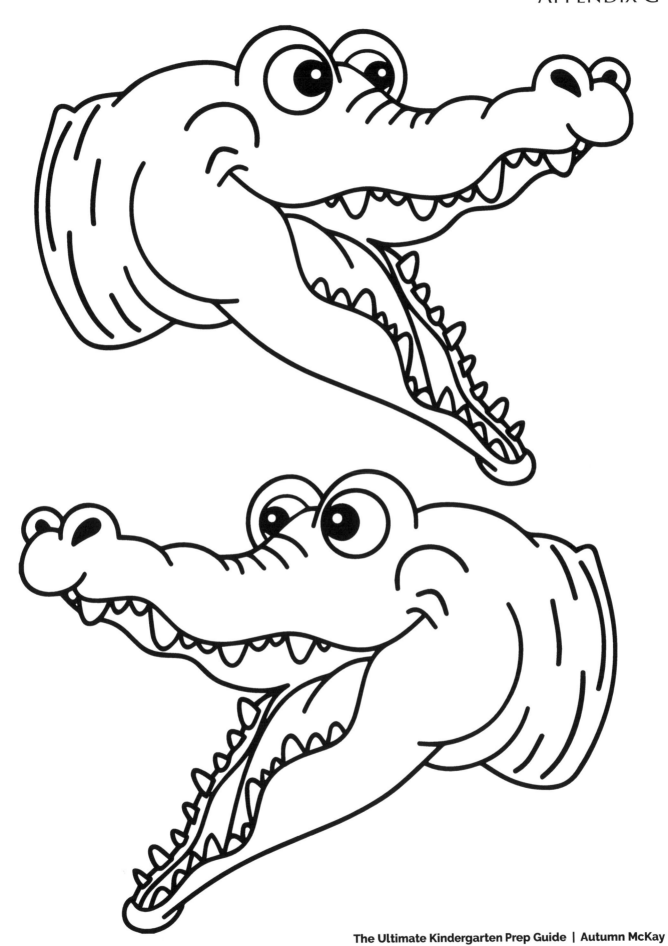

1 7

9 4

2 6

8 5

10 3

More or Less

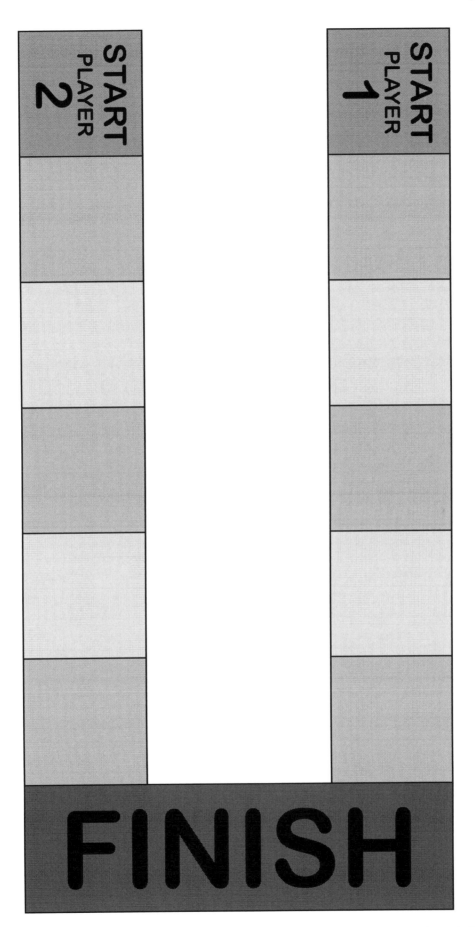

START
PLAYER
2

START
PLAYER
1

FINISH

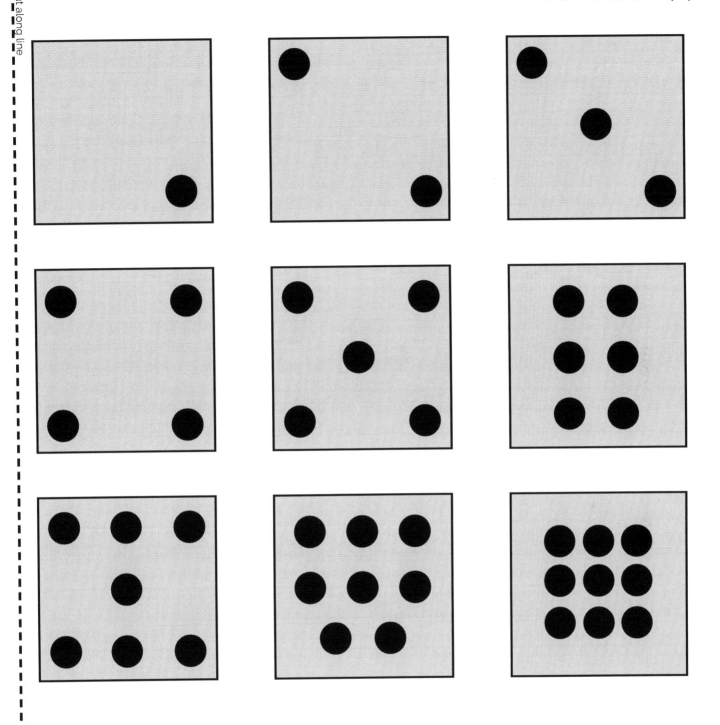

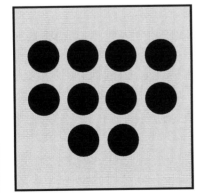

cut along line

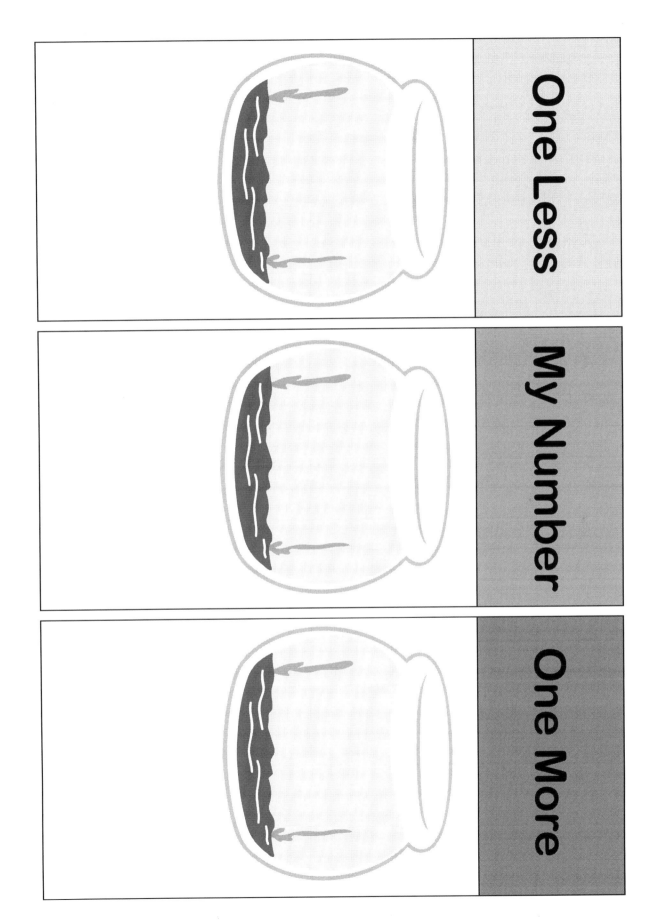

One Less

My Number

One More

cut along line

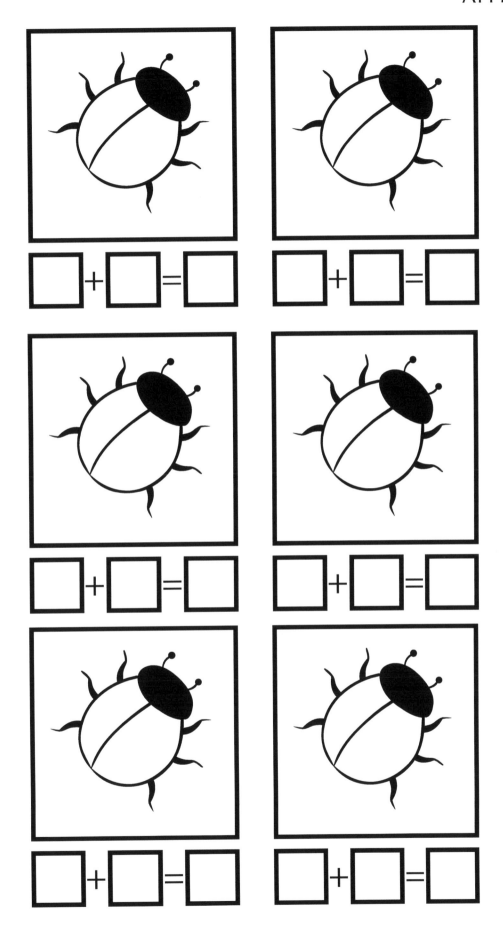

cut along line

Say it

Make it

Answer it

0 1 2 3 4 5 6 7 8 9 10

 Start at 2 and hop forward 3 spaces.

 Start at 6 and hop forward 2 spaces.

 Start at 1 and hop forward 5 spaces.

 Start at 3 and hop forward 4 spaces.

 Start at _____ and hop forward _____ spaces.

 Start at 10 and hop back 5 spaces.

 Start at 4 and hop back 4 spaces.

 Start at 9 and hop back 1 spaces.

 Start at 6 and hop back 3 spaces.

 Start at _____ and hop back _____ spaces.

cut along line

The Ultimate Kindergarten Prep Guide | Autumn McKay

Read it

Draw it

Answer it

My mom made 6 pancakes for breakfast.
I ate 2. How many are left?

One butterfly lands on a bush.
Then 3 more butterflies join him.
How many butterflies are on the bush?

The book has 10 pages in it.
I've read 8. How many pages are left
to read?

I build 5 tall towers. My friend builds
4 tall towers. How many tall towers
did we build altogether?

There are 9 seats on the bus.
Six students each take a seat on the bus.
How many seats are left?

The Falcons have 2 touchdowns.
They get 2 more touchdowns. How many
touchdowns did they have altogether?

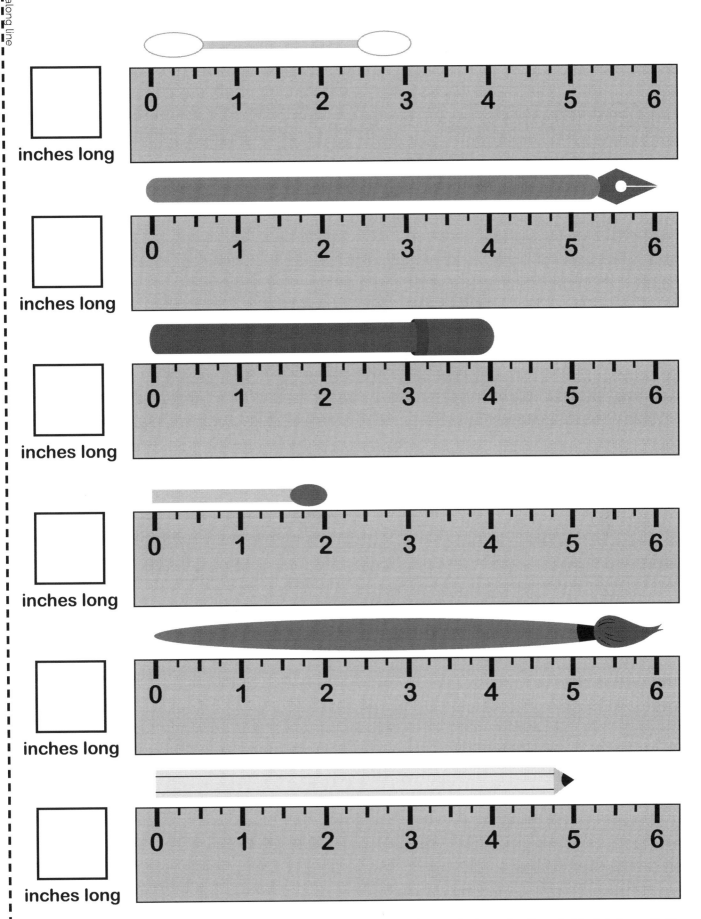

inches long

inches long

inches long

inches long

inches long

inches long

Cut out the sunflowers and paste them in order from shortest to tallest

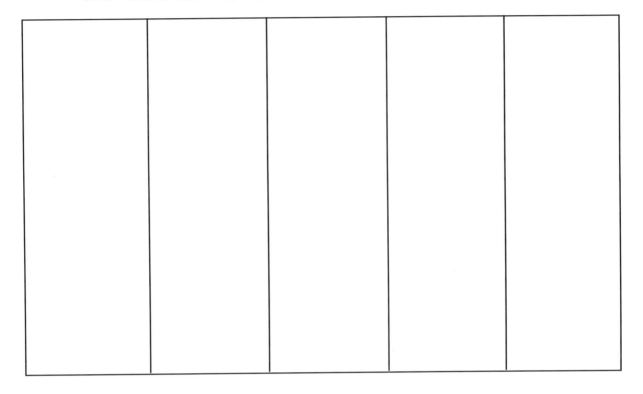

cut along line

Family Member	Height

🦋 I am _____ inches tall.

🦋 I am taller than _____.

🦋 Im shorter than _____.

🦋 The tallest family member in our house is _____.

🦋 The shortest family member in our house is _____.

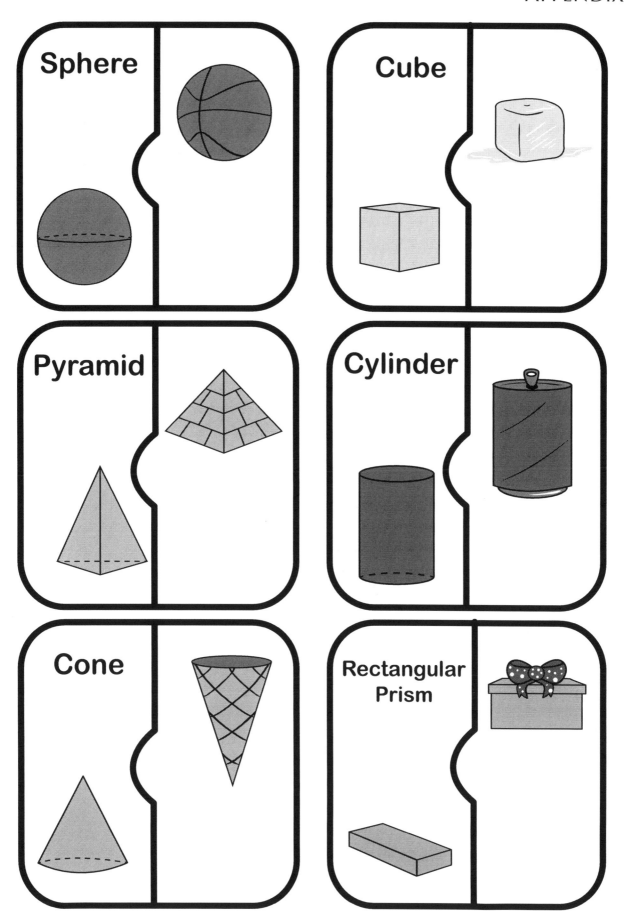

Sphere

Cube

Pyramid

Cylinder

Cone

Rectangular Prism

cut along line

cut along line

Look for this shape	Draw a picture of the object you found
Circle	
Square	
Triangle	
Rectangle	
Oval	
Cone	
Cube	
Sphere	
Rectangular Prism	
Cylinder	

My Shape Character

Shapes I Used

Circle

Oval

Octagon

Triangle

Square

Rectangle

Diamond

cut along line

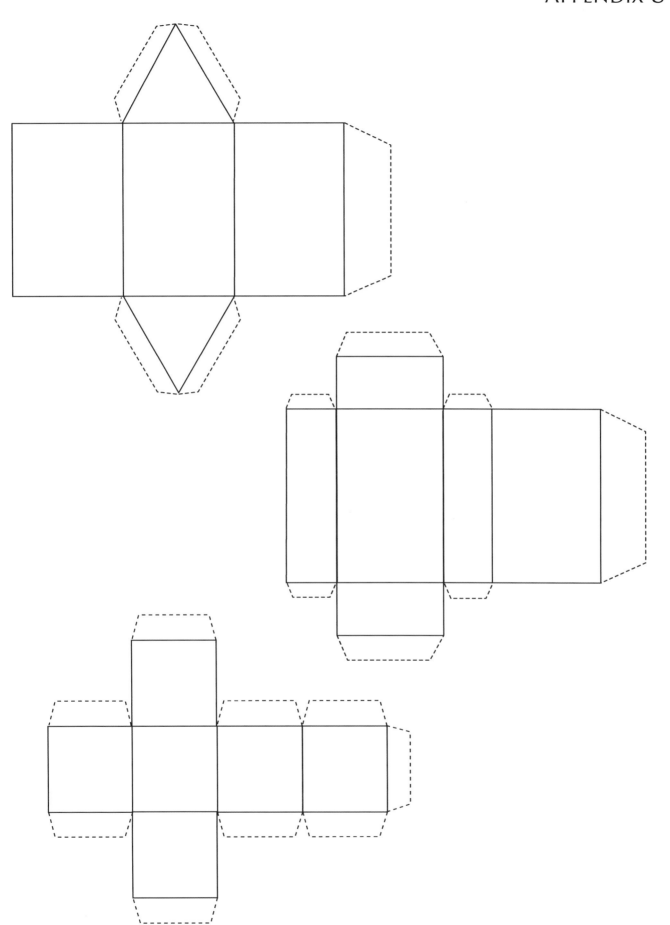

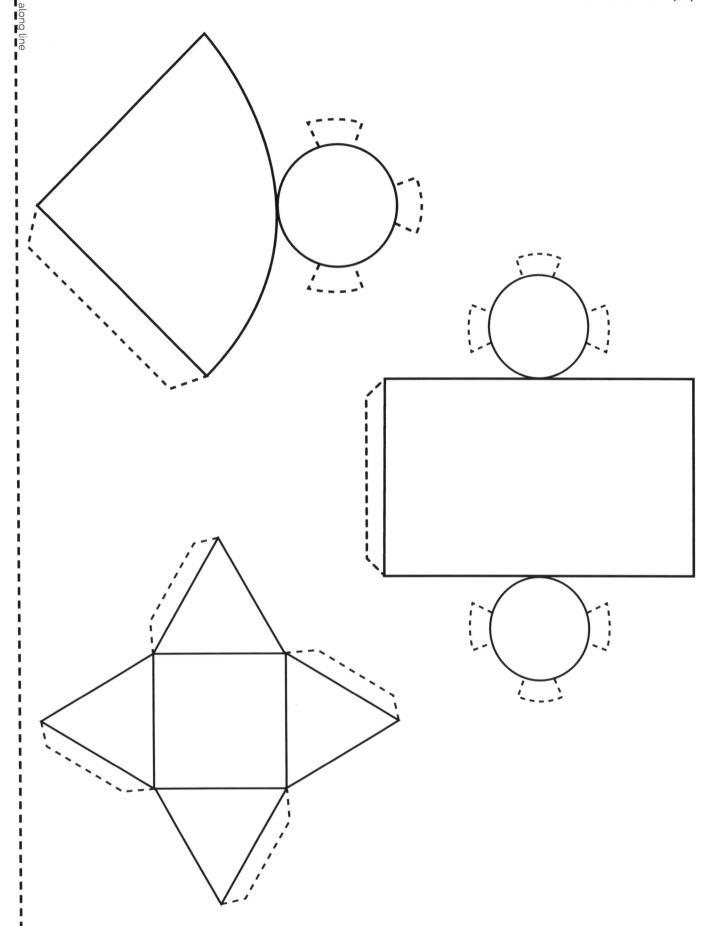

Raise your arms ABOVE your head

Touch the TOP of your head

Touch the BOTTOM of your foot

Stand NEXT to... (fill in with object)

Walk AROUND... (fill in with object)

Hold UP your right hand

Kick your LEFT leg

Stand BESIDE me

Stand in FRONT of the door

Get a toy OFF a shelf

Jump UP

Put your hand ON a book

Get BEHIND... (fill in with object)

Walk THROUGH the doorway

Look UNDER... (fill in with object)

Pick up something NEAR you

Look INSIDE... (fill in with object)

Get DOWN on the ground

cut along line

cut along line

LETTER

WORD

SENTENCE

cut along line

T

SUN

I see a dog.

CAR

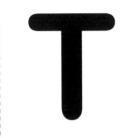
CAT

G

I can run.

The bus can go.

A

MUG

I have a ball.

W

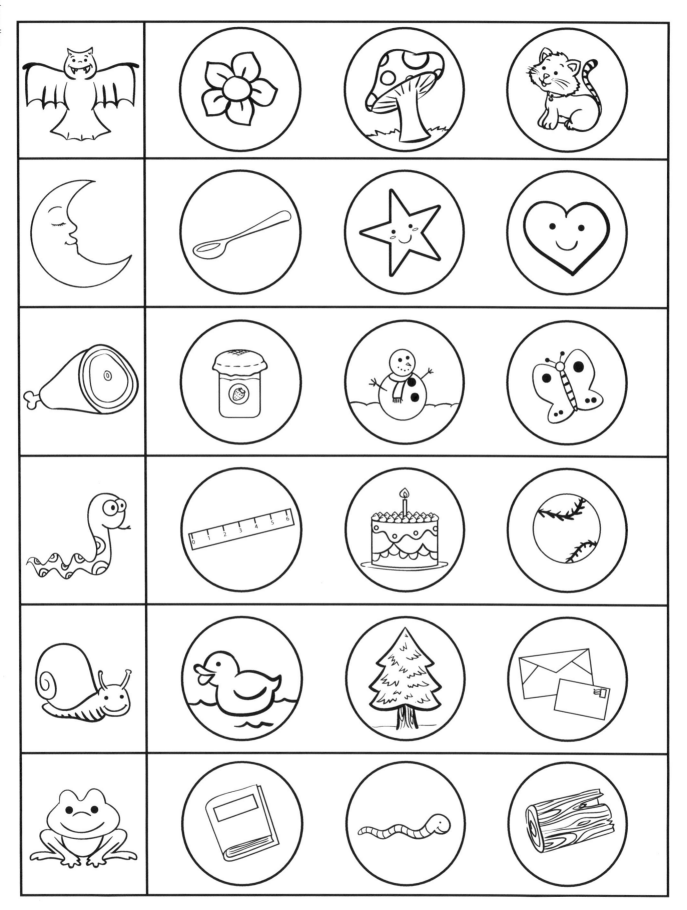

cut along line

Frog

Dog

Rake

Cake

Cat

Rat

Fox

Box

Tree

cut along line

Bee

Can

Fan

Honey

Money

Duck

Truck

Clock

Sock

cut along line

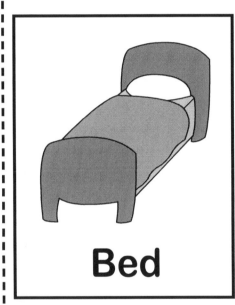

Bed

Sled

cut along line

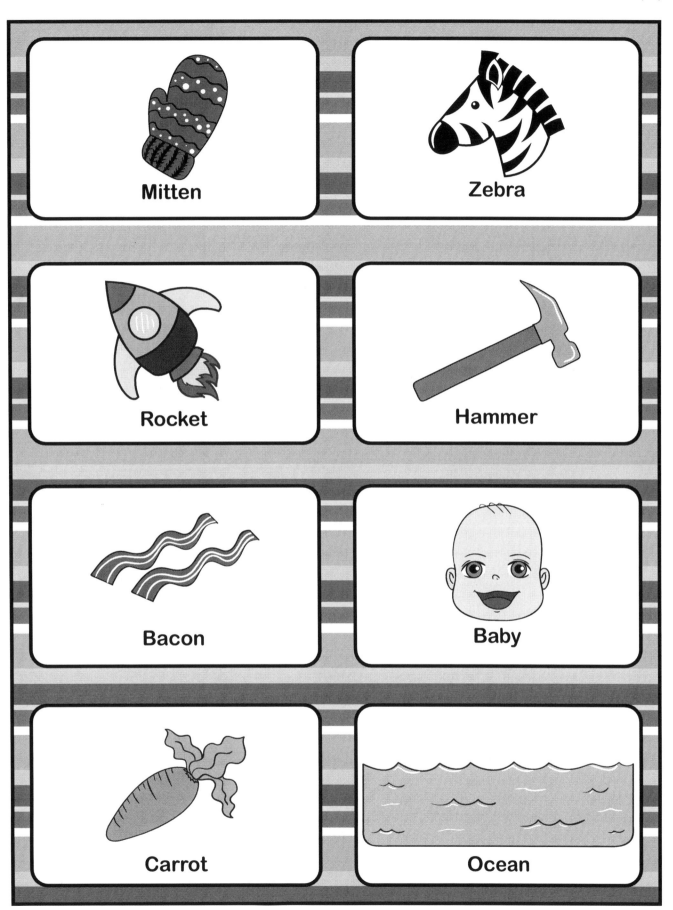

Mitten

Zebra

Rocket

Hammer

Bacon

Baby

Carrot

Ocean

cut along line

Bumblebee

Computer

Basketball

Spaghetti

Ladybug

Bicycle

Umbrella

Elephant

cut along line

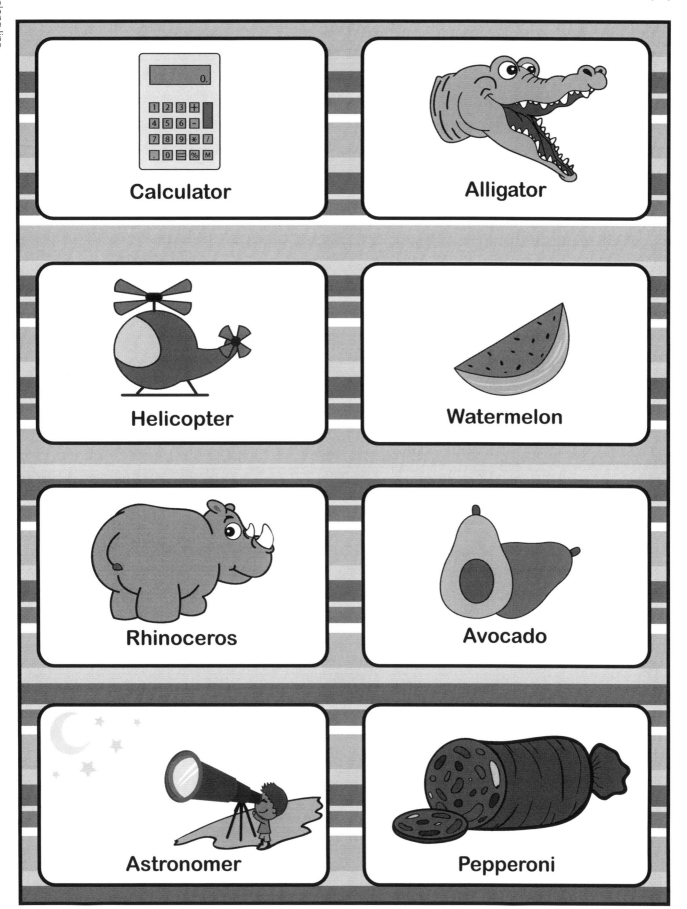

Calculator

Alligator

Helicopter

Watermelon

Rhinoceros

Avocado

Astronomer

Pepperoni

cut along line

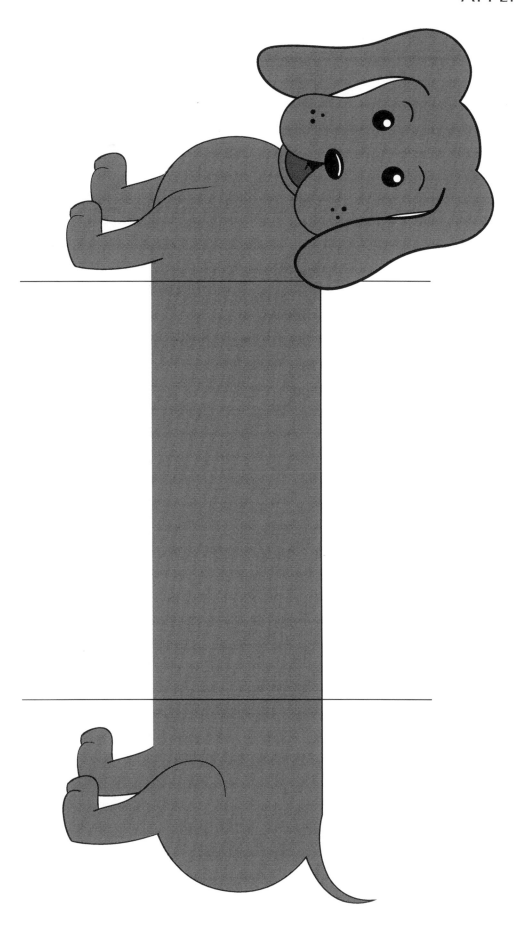

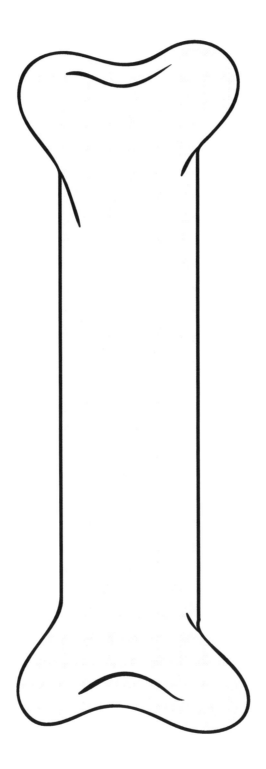

The little Pig

By Darren Smith
Illustrated by CyAn Platas

TITLE	AUTHOR	ILLUSTRATOR
SPINE	FRONT COVER	BACK COVER

cut along line

cut along line

Cut and paste the non-fiction books here.

Cut and paste the fiction books here.

Write your own title for a non-fiction and a fiction book.

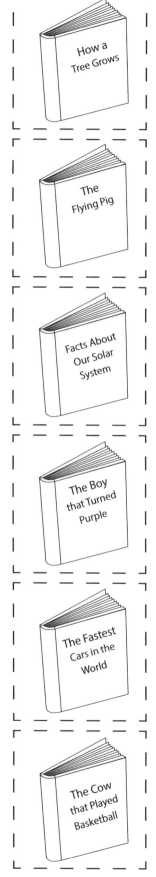

How a Tree Grows

The Flying Pig

Facts About Our Solar System

The Boy that Turned Purple

The Fastest Cars in the World

The Cow that Played Basketball

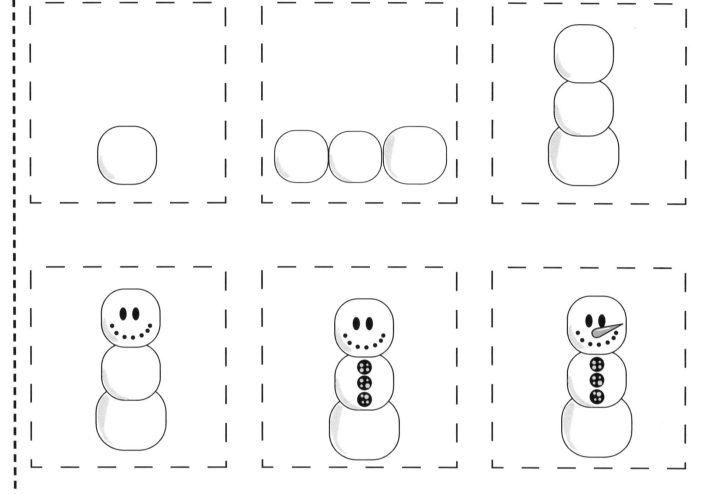

cut along line

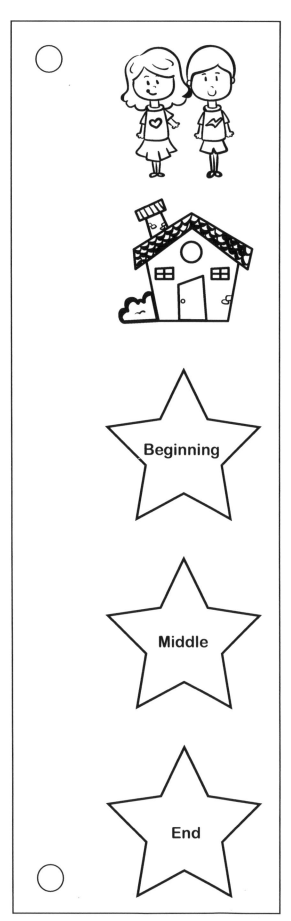

cut along line

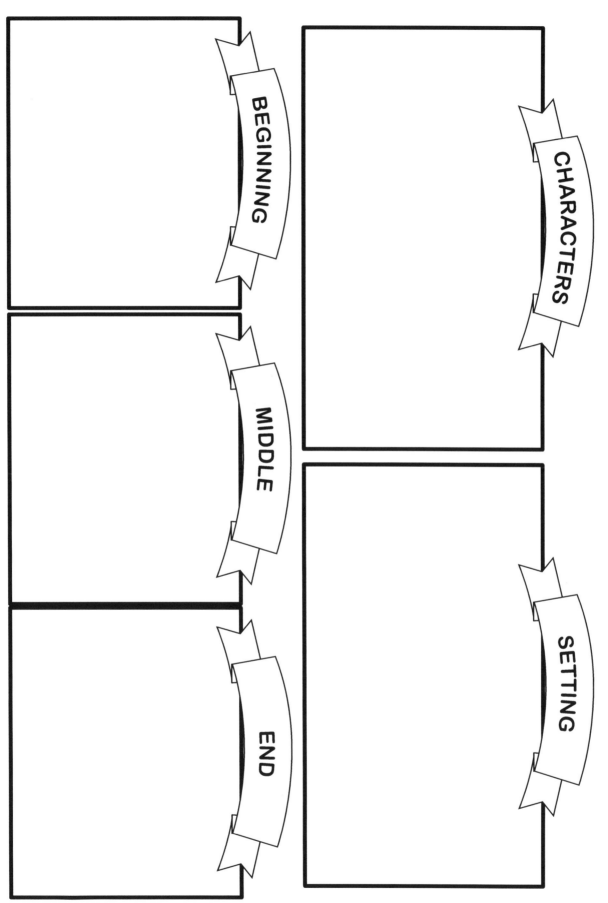

BEGINNING

MIDDLE

END

CHARACTERS

SETTING

cut along line

cut along line

WHAT?

WHEN?

WHERE?

WHO?

1

2

3

4

5

6

A	B	C	D	E	F	G
A	B	C	D	E	F	G

H	I	J	K	L	M	N
H	I	J	K	L	M	N

O	P	Q	R	S	T	U
O	P	Q	R	S	T	U

V	W	X	Y	Z
V	W	X	Y	Z

a	b	c	d	e	f	g
a	b	c	d	e	f	g

h	i	j	k	l	m	n
h	i	j	k	l	m	n

o	p	q	r	s	t	u
o	p	q	r	s	t	u

v	w	x	y	z
v	w	x	y	z

cut along line

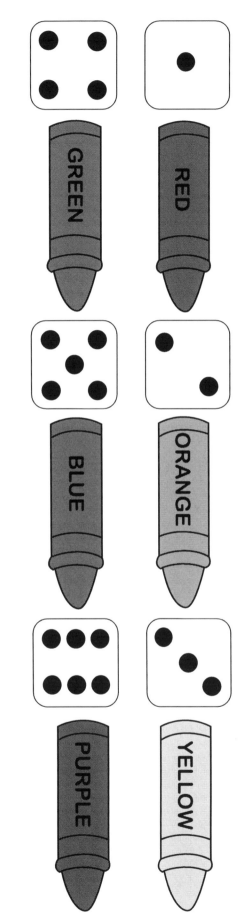

cut along line

The Ultimate Kindergarten Prep Guide | Autumn McKay

cut along line

see   I   cat   a

HOT

COLD

AWAKE

ASLEEP

SHORT

TALL

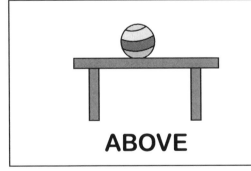

ABOVE

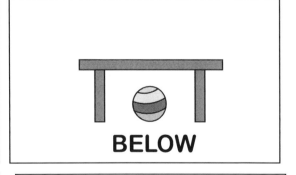

BELOW

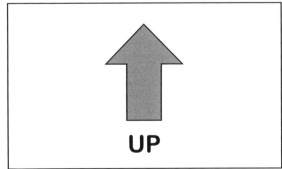

UP

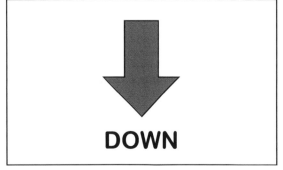

DOWN

cut along line

cut along line

cut along line

SHOUT	LARGE
FUNNY	FINISH
FAST	SILLY
TINY	QUICK
END	TIDY
CLEAN	GLAD
HAPPY	YELL
BIG	LITTLE

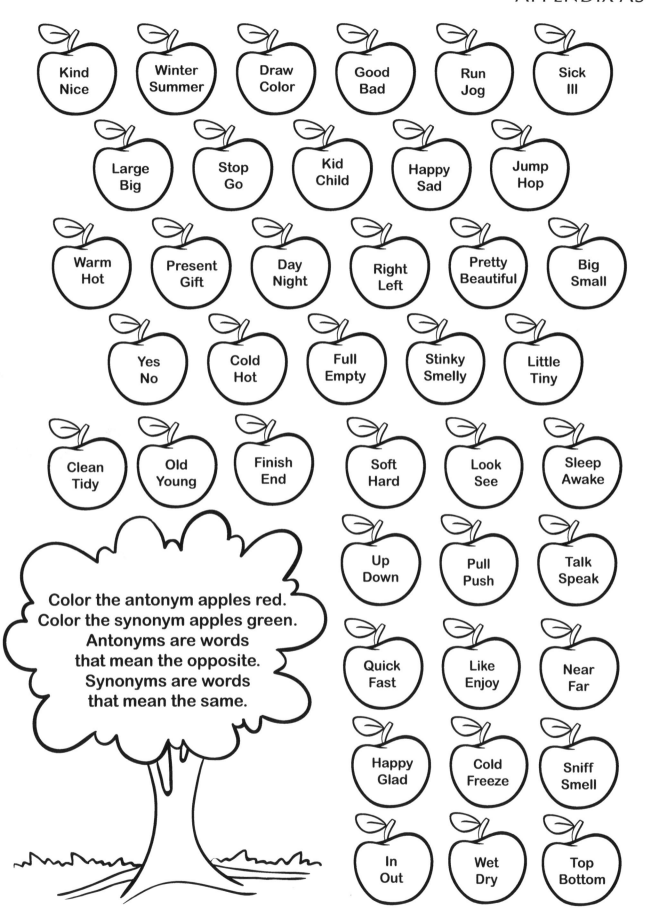

Kind
Nice

Winter
Summer

Draw
Color

Good
Bad

Run
Jog

Sick
Ill

Large
Big

Stop
Go

Kid
Child

Happy
Sad

Jump
Hop

Warm
Hot

Present
Gift

Day
Night

Right
Left

Pretty
Beautiful

Big
Small

Yes
No

Cold
Hot

Full
Empty

Stinky
Smelly

Little
Tiny

Clean
Tidy

Old
Young

Finish
End

Soft
Hard

Look
See

Sleep
Awake

Up
Down

Pull
Push

Talk
Speak

Quick
Fast

Like
Enjoy

Near
Far

Happy
Glad

Cold
Freeze

Sniff
Smell

In
Out

Wet
Dry

Top
Bottom

Color the antonym apples red.
Color the synonym apples green.
Antonyms are words
that mean the opposite.
Synonyms are words
that mean the same.

cut along line

SHIP

BAT

FLY

WAVE

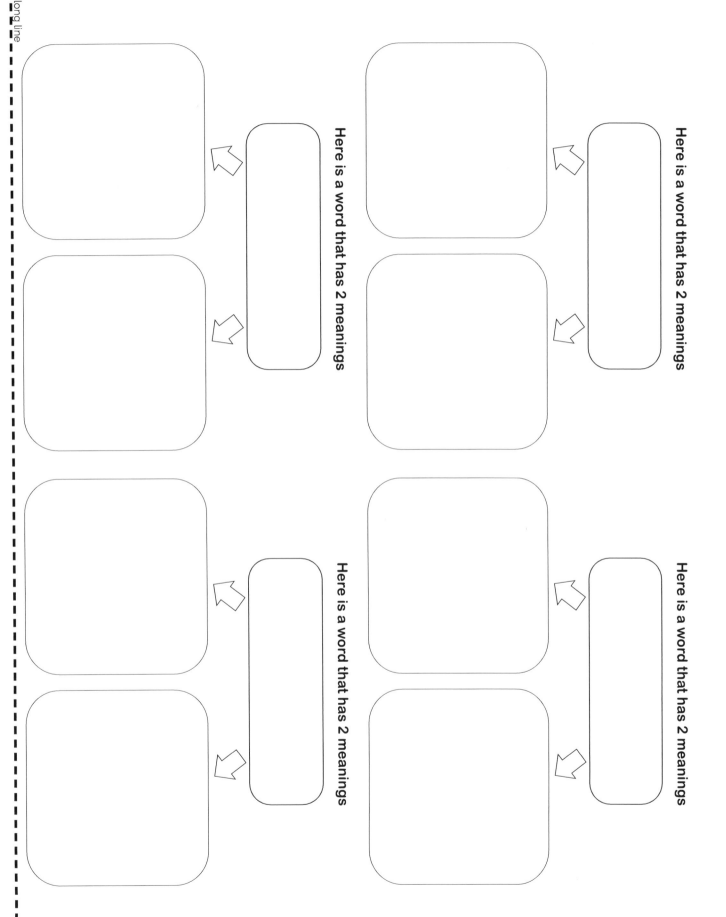

Here is a word that has 2 meanings

Here is a word that has 2 meanings

Here is a word that has 2 meanings

Here is a word that has 2 meanings

cut along line

Can I read the book	(.) (?) (!)
The dog is big	(.) (?) (!)
I have three bananas	(.) (?) (!)
Ouch, that hurt	(.) (?) (!)
Is it going to snow	(.) (?) (!)
The sun is big and yellow	(.) (?) (!)
What time is it	(.) (?) (!)
Wow, look at that	(.) (?) (!)

cut along line

Correct the Sentence

i   see the bird.

t   he boy is fast.

s   he can swim.

l   ook at the yellow bus.

d   uke, the dog, wants a treat.

I   S   D   L   T

cut along line

Read It, Fix It, Draw It!

Circle the first letter in the sentence.
Rewrite the sentence correctly.
Then draw a picture to match.

the frog hopped

 # Day or Night?

Cut and paste the pictures in the correct box.

Day

Night

cut along line

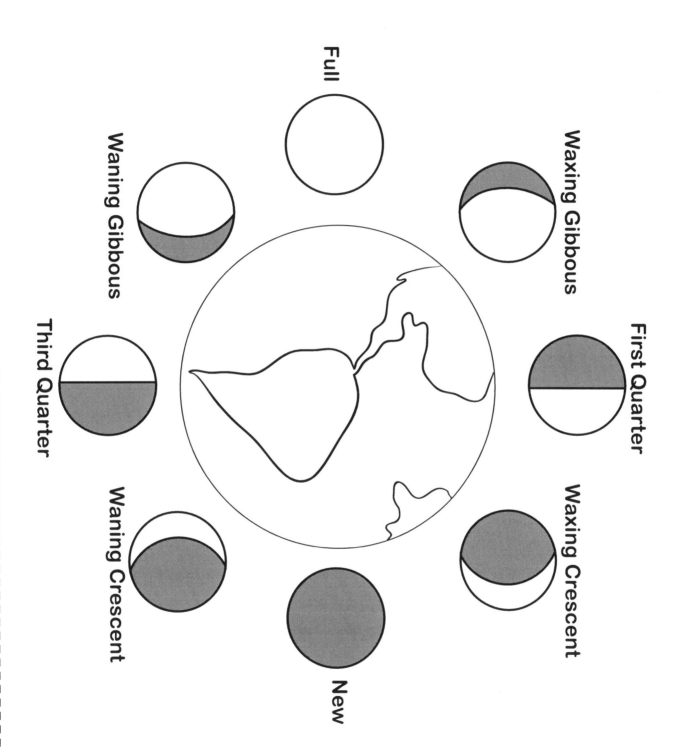

cut along line

Planets

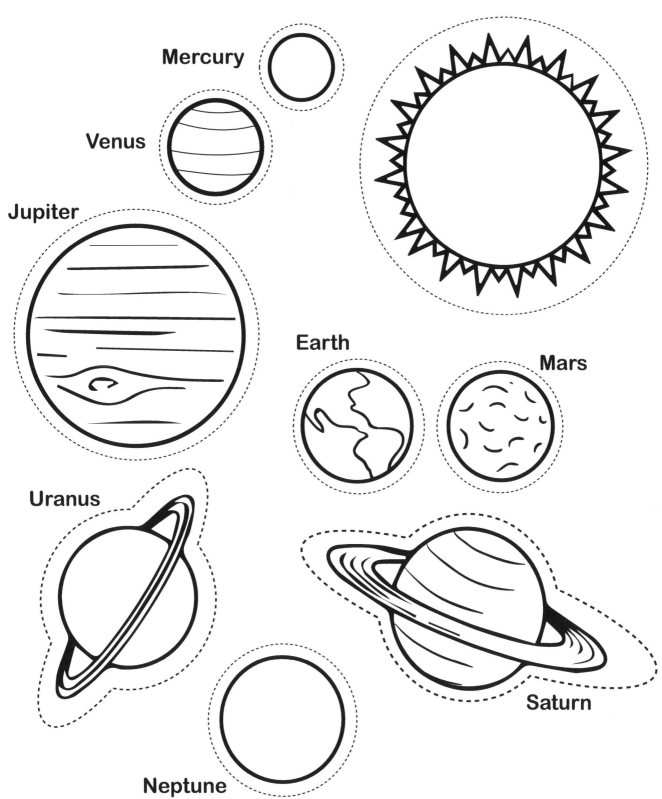

Mercury

Venus

Jupiter

Earth

Mars

Uranus

Saturn

Neptune

cut along line

Fabric

Paper

Wood

Plastic

Glass

Metal

cut along line

Sink or Float?

Type of Candy	Prediction	Result

cut along line

Goldfish vs. Goldfish Cracker

	GOLDFISH	GOLDFISH CRACKER
Does it move on its own?		
Does it need food and water?		
Does it make more of itself?		
Does it grow and change?		
Does it need air?		

Which one is living? _____

Explain why the _____ is living.

cut along line

cut along line

Living	Nonliving

cut along line

Vertebrate	Invertebrate

Mammals

Mammals are a group of animals that live on land, at sea, in the air, and under the ground. Mammals are warm-blooded which means they can make their own body heat even when it's cold outside. Mammals have hair or fur. Mammals give birth to live babies, and feed their babies with milk.

1. Mammals are
  a. Warm-blooded
  b. Cold-blooded
  c. No-blooded

2. Mammals have hair or _____

3. Mammals live on land, at sea, in the air, and
  a. On top of houses
  b. Under the ground
  c. In outer space

4. Mammals feed their babies _____

5. Color the mammals.

cut along line

Life Cycle of a Frog

cut along line

Animal Body Coverings

Glue the correct texture into each Animal Covering box.
Then draw an example of each animal in the Example box

Animal Group	Animal Covering	Example
Mammals		
Reptiles		
Amphibians		
Birds		
Fish		

Plant Parts

Plant Needs

| Seeds | Sunlight | Leaves | Water |

| Fruit | Flower | Air | Soil |

| Stem | Roots |

cut along line

What Effects Plant Growth?

Fill in the name of the liquids used to water each plant. Each day, use a ruler to measure the plants' growth. Write the measurement in the chart.

Type of Liquid Used	Day 1	Day 2	Day 3	Day 4	Day 5	Day 6	Day 7

cut along line

Flag of the United States

The picture below shows the American flag.
It is the flag for the United States of America.
Betty Ross designed the first U.S. flag.

The flag's colors are red, white and blue.
• Red is a symbol for bravery.
• Blue is a symbol for justice and mindfulness.
• White is a symbol for purity and innocence.

There are 50 white stars against a blue background.
Each star represents one of the 50 states in our country.
There are 13 red and white stripes on the American flag.
The top and bottom stripes are both red.
The 13 stripes represent the 13 original colonies that became states
when America was first started.

Color the flag below by using the correct colors.

cut along line

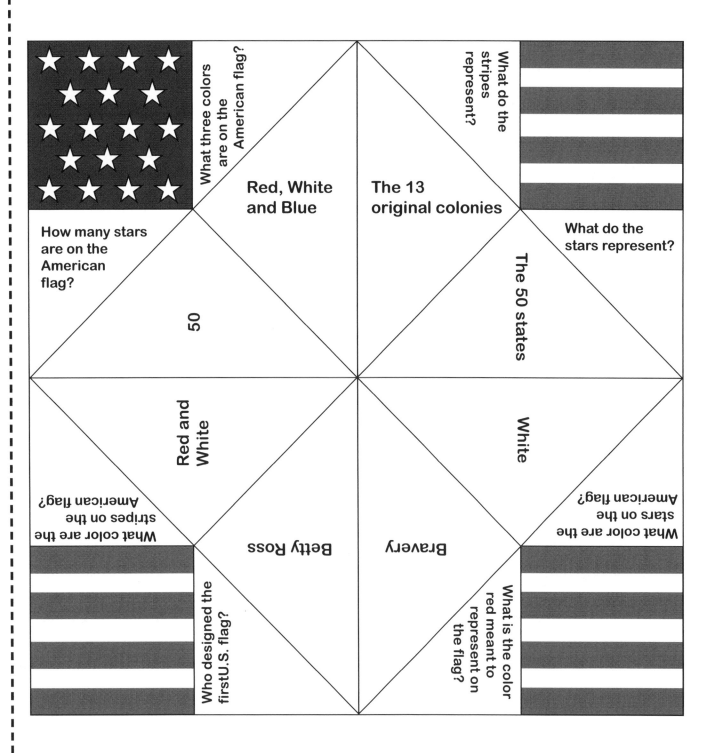

What three colors are on the American flag?

What do the stripes represent?

Red, White and Blue

The 13 original colonies

How many stars are on the American flag?

What do the stars represent?

50

The 50 states

Red and White

White

What color are the stripes on the American flag?

What color are the stars on the American flag?

Betty Ross

Bravery

Who designed the first U.S. flag?

What is the color red meant to represent on the flag?

Pledge of Allegiance

I | _____ | ALLEGIANCE TO THE | _____ |

OF THE UNITED STATES OF | _____ | , AND TO THE

| _____ | FOR WHICH IT STANDS, ONE | _____ |

UNDER GOD, INDIVISIBLE WITH | _____ | AND

| _____ | FOR ALL.

| PLEDGE | | FLAG | | AMERICA | | REPUBLIC |

| NATION | | LIBERTY | | JUSTICE |

Star-Spangled Banner

```
S F I Y K P O D Y R
E L K Y E D E I R E
P A D A Q L U Q O N
I G C S G S E V T N
R E M N E E R F C A
T Q A B E M O H I B
S P C E R G B P V S
S L A N D A L G X T
T E K C O R V E C A
U G H H S B J E S R
```

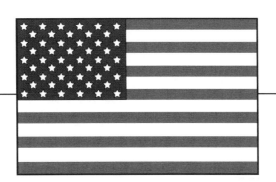

BANNER	BRAVE	FLAG
FREE	HOME	LAND
PEACE	ROCKET	SPANGLED
STAR	STRIPES	VICTORY

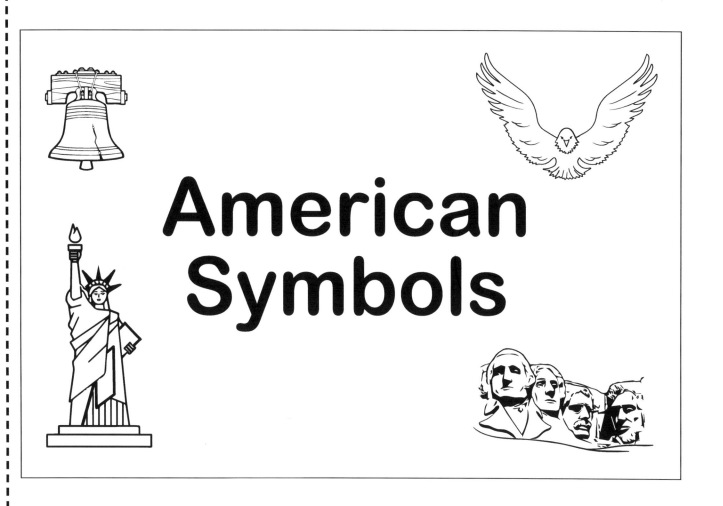

American Symbols

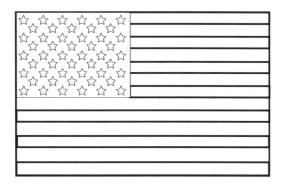

American Flag

The United States of America flag is red, white, and blue.
It has 50 stars and 13 stripes.

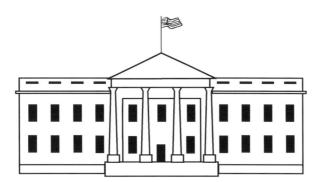

The White House

The President of the United States lives in the White House.
It was built between 1792 and 1800.

Statue of Liberty

The Statue of Liberty was a gift from France.
The statue is in New York,
and she welcomes people to the United States.

Bald Eagle

The bald eagle represents freedom.
It is the emblem of the United States of America.

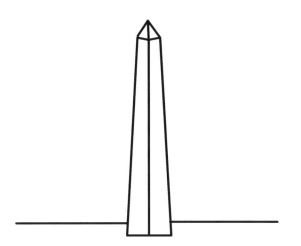

Washington Monument

The Washington Monument was built to remember
our first President, George Washington.
The Washington Monument is in Washington D.C.

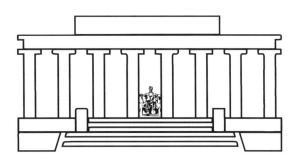

Lincoln Memorial

The Lincoln Memorial was built to honor our 16th President,
Abraham Lincoln. The Lincoln Memorial is in Washington D.C.

cut along line

cut along line

Liberty Bell

The Liberty Bell is a symbol of America's independence. The Liberty Bell cracked the first time it was rung. It is located in Philadelphia, Pennsylvania.

Mount Rushmore

Mount Rushmore is a mountain with the faces of former presidents Theodore Roosevelt, Abraham Lincoln, Thomas Jefferson, and George Washington. It is located in South Dakota.

Yesterday and Tomorrow

Yesterday	Today	Tomorrow
	Sunday	
	Monday	
	Tuesday	
	Wednesday	
	Thursday	
	Friday	
	Saturday	

Sunday	Monday	Tuesday
Wednesday		Thursday
Friday		Saturday

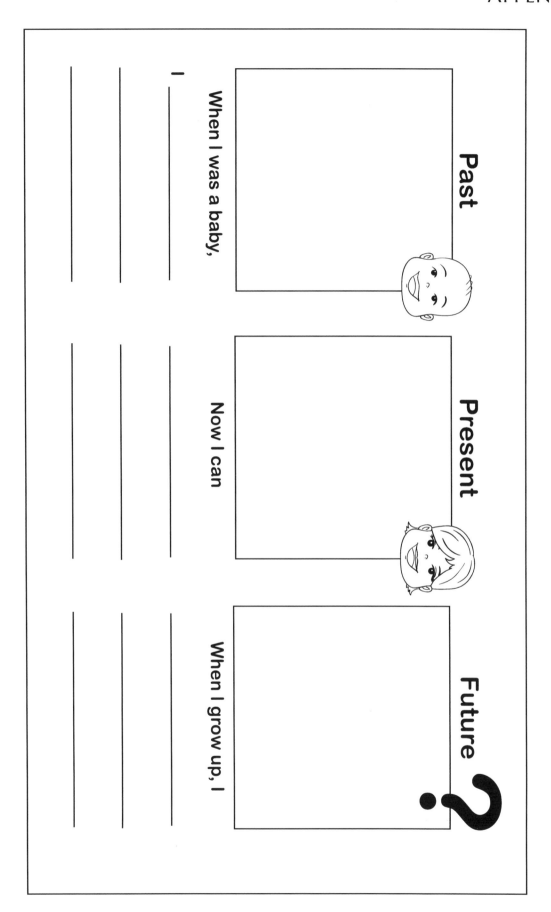

Past

When I was a baby,

Present

Now I can

Future ?

When I grow up, I

Long Ago	Now

Everyone walks to school

Car

Computer

Telephone

Feather Pen

Candlelight

Watch

Cell Phone

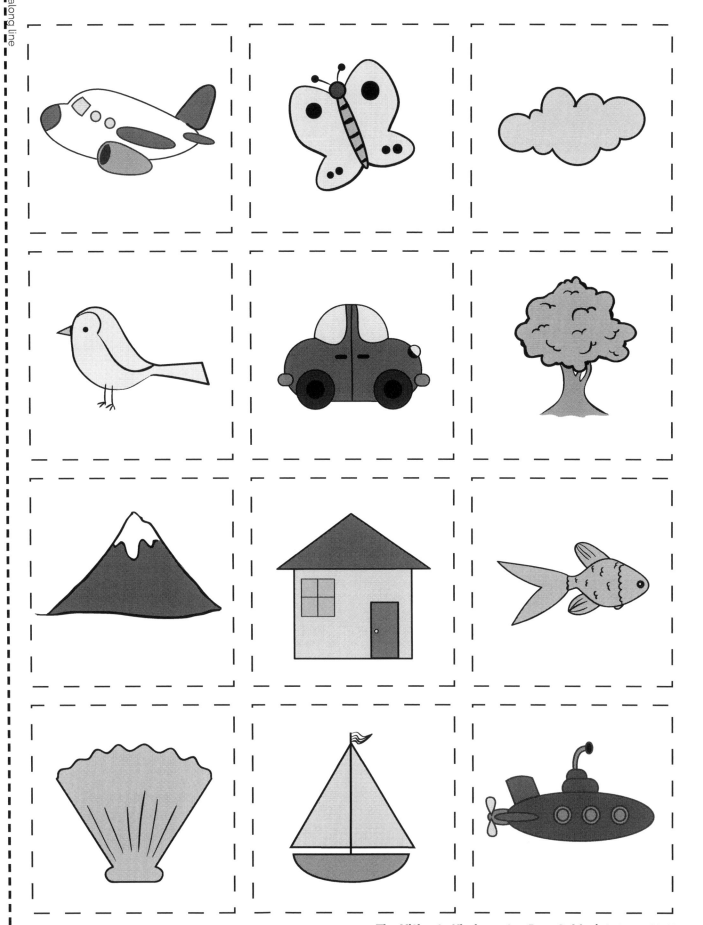

cut along line

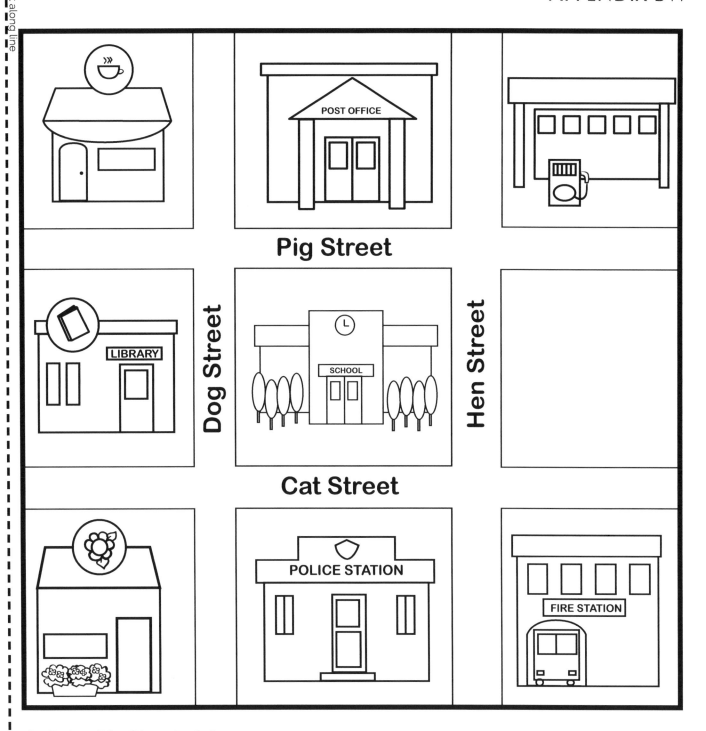

Pig Street

Dog Street

Hen Street

Cat Street

LIBRARY

POST OFFICE

SCHOOL

POLICE STATION

FIRE STATION

cut along line

1- Color Pig Street pink.

2- Color Hen Street yellow.

3- Draw a car on Cat Street.

4- Color Dog Street brown.

5- Color the Police Station blue.

6- Draw a tree next to the Post Office.

7- Draw a house in an available spot on Hen Street.

8- Color the flower in the Flower Shop.

9- Color Cat Street orange.

My Home

My Street

cut along line

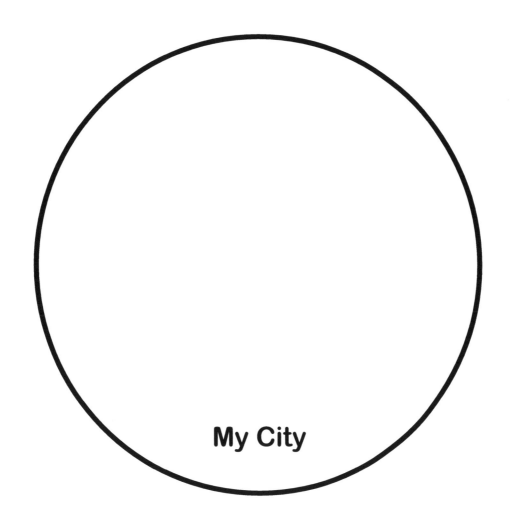

My City

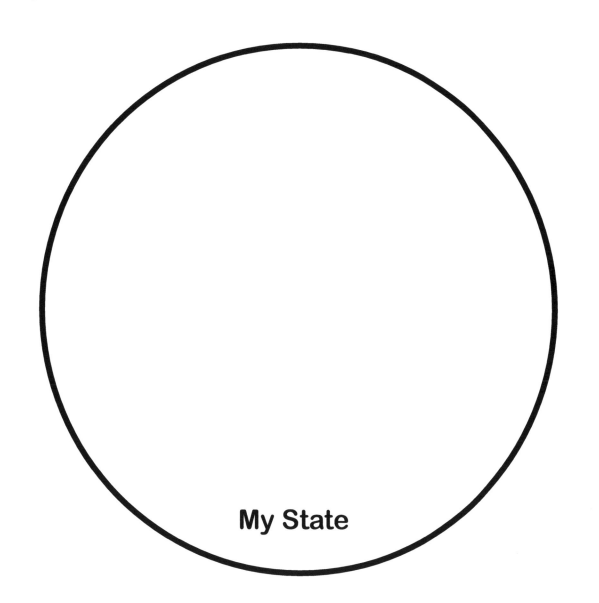

My State

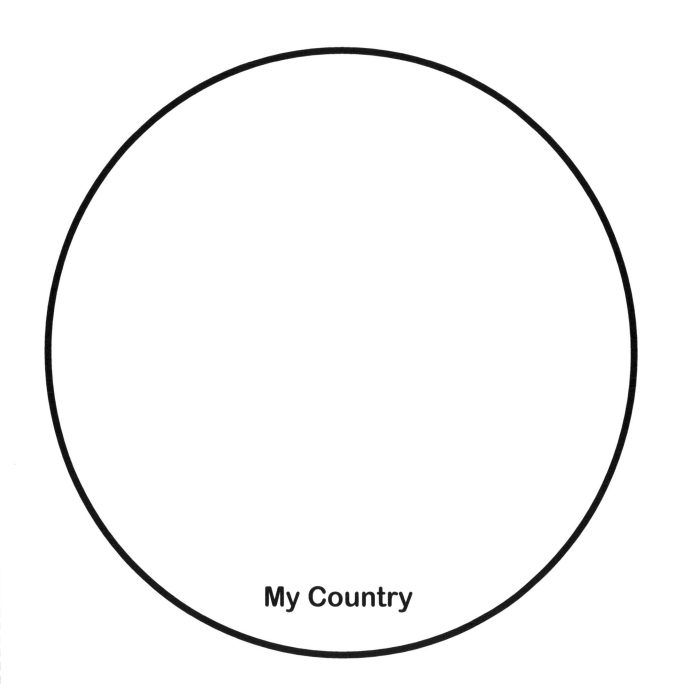

My Country

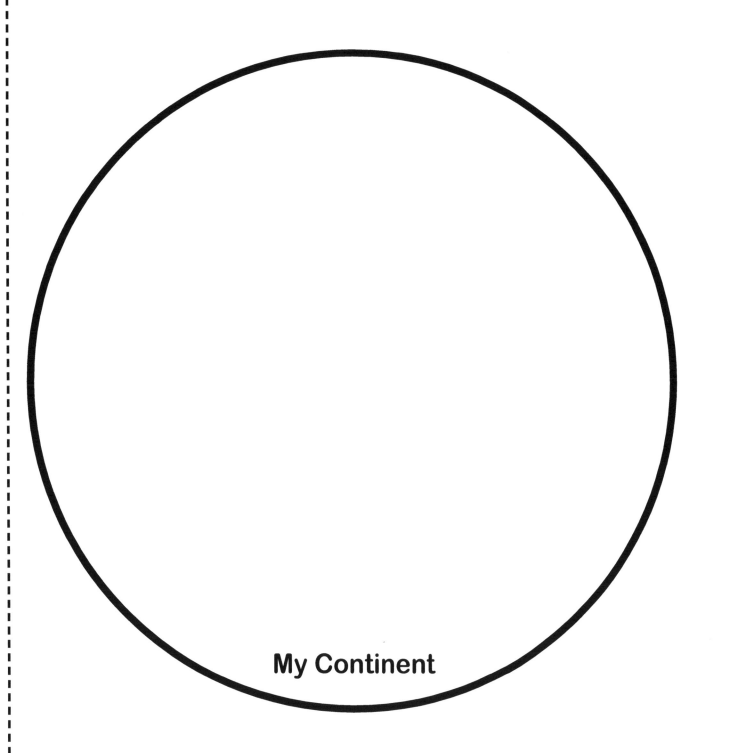

My Continent

My Planet

VOTE FOR ME

Voter Registration Application

What is your name?

_____

- -

_____

1- Do you work hard?

☐ YES ☐ NO

2- Are you kind to others?

☐ YES ☐ NO

3- Do you listen to your parents?

☐ YES ☐ NO

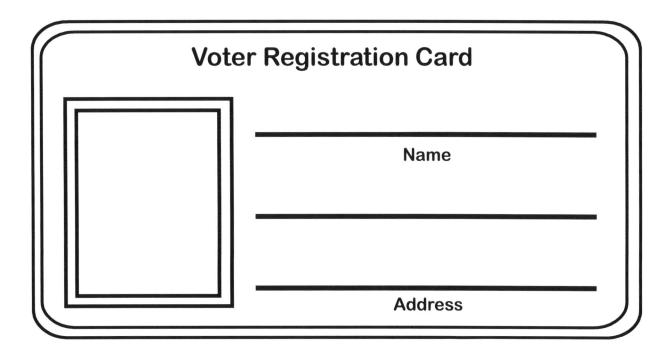

Voter Registration Card

_____

Name

_____

Address

Let's Make an Informed Decision

_____

Ballot

Election Results

Tally up the votes

Graph the results

Goods	Services

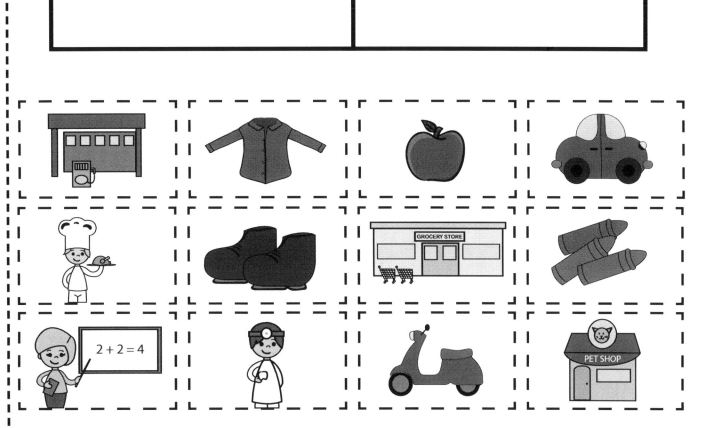

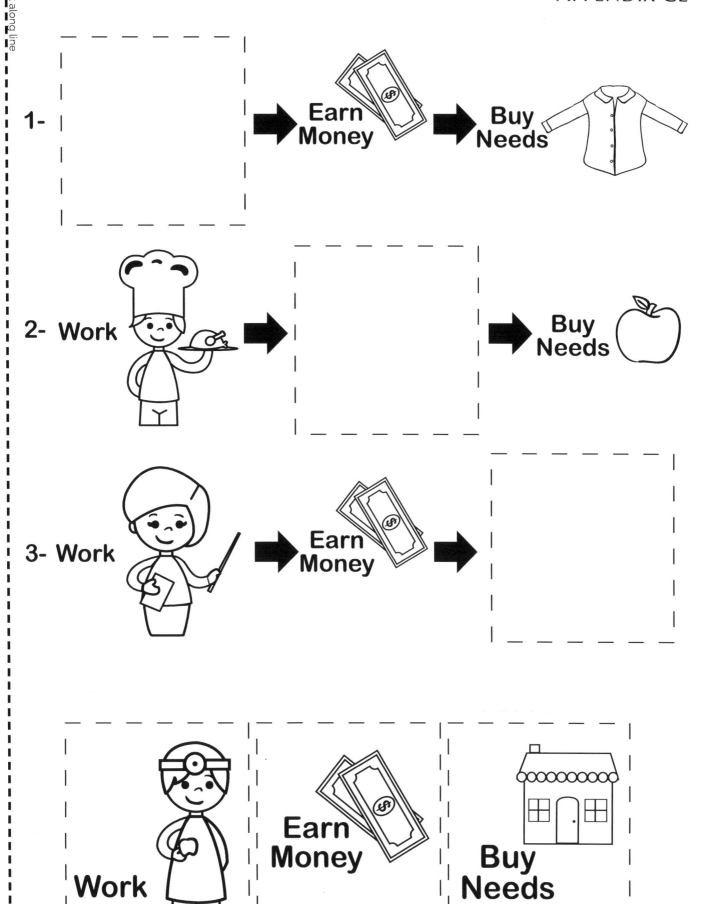

1-   → **Earn Money** → **Buy Needs**

2- Work   →   → **Buy Needs**

3- Work   → **Earn Money** →

Work   Earn Money   Buy Needs

cut along line

cut along line

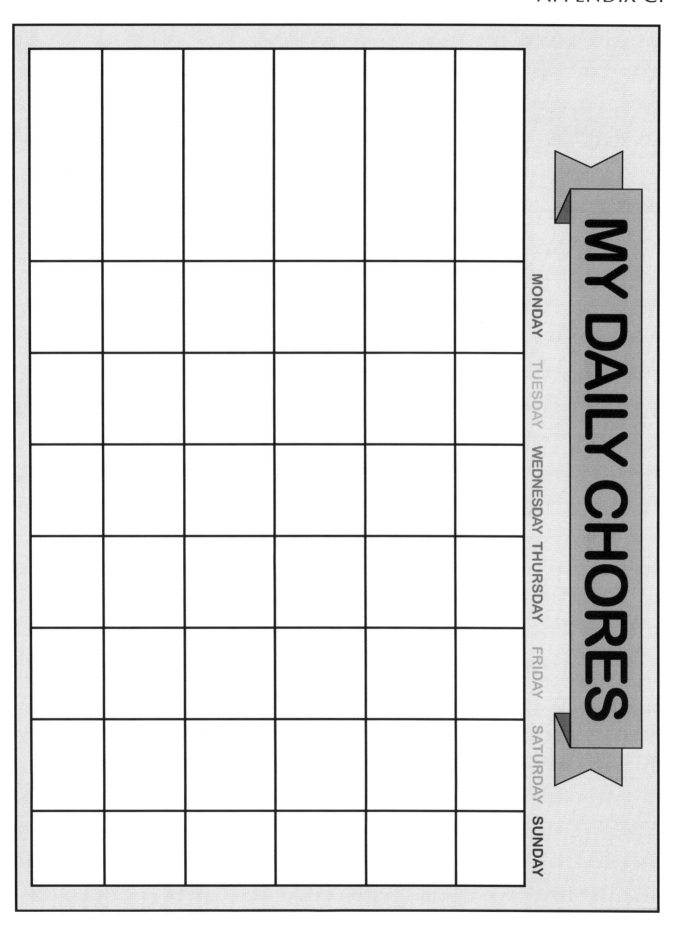

MY DAILY CHORES

MONDAY TUESDAY WEDNESDAY THURSDAY FRIDAY SATURDAY SUNDAY

My Business

My business is called _____

I sell goods / services / both . (Circle one)

Customers come to my business to _____

_____

My customers are _____

Here is a picture of my business:

Grocery List

Budget: _____

_____

_____

_____

_____

_____

_____

_____

_____

_____

Grocery List

Budget: _____

_____

_____

_____

_____

_____

_____

_____

_____

_____

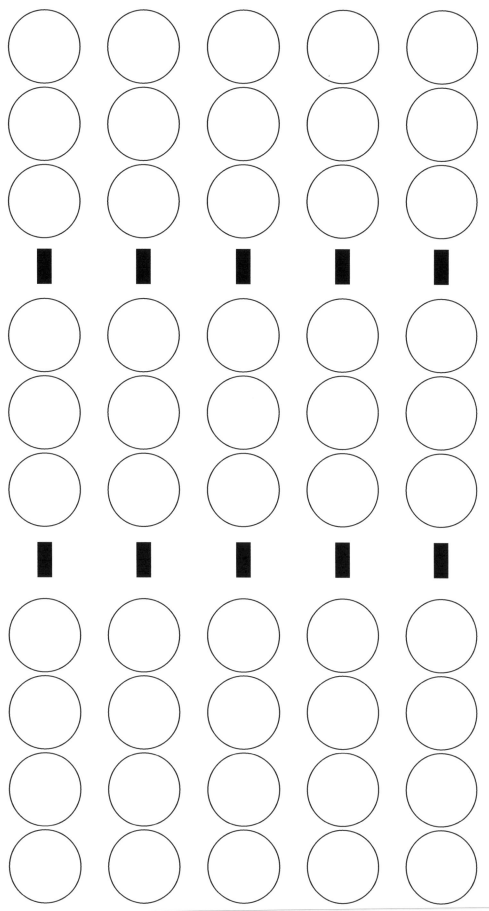

Phone Number Stickers

cut along line

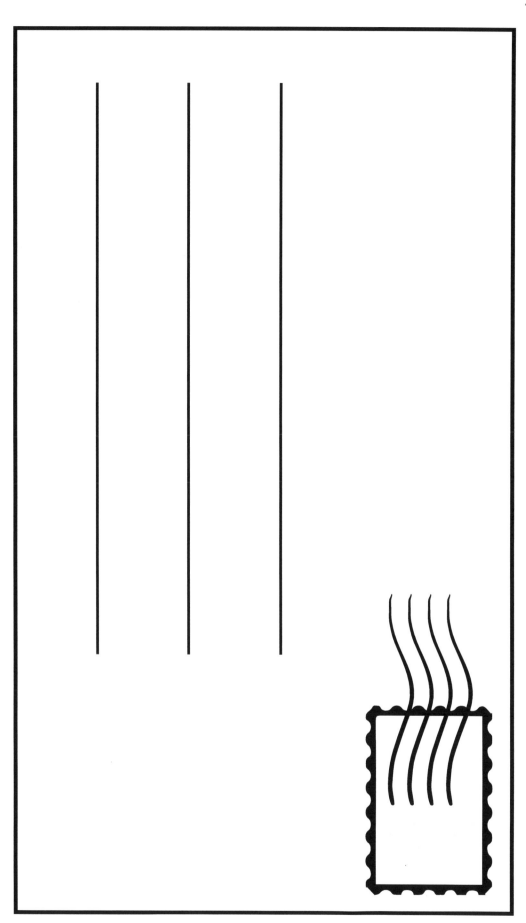

I know my address!

cut along line

Thank you for welcoming me into your home!
I hope you and your child liked learning together with this book!

If you enjoyed this book, it would mean so much to me
if you wrote a review so other moms can learn from your
experience.

-♡-
Autumn

Autumn@BestMomIdeas.com

Discover Autumn's Other Books

Early Learning Series

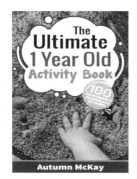

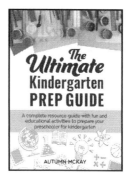

Early Learning Workbook Series

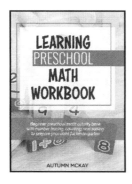

Made in the USA
Las Vegas, NV
28 October 2021